JEAN M

AUDITION SPEECHES
for MEN

A & C Black • London

To
BRIAN SCHWARTZ
'Thank you'

First published in 2001
Reprinted 2004
A & C Black Publishers Limited
37 Soho Square, London W1D 3QZ
www.acblack.com

© 2001 Jean Marlow

ISBN 0-7136-5285-3

A CIP catalogue record for this book is available from the
British Library

A & C Black uses paper produced with elemental chorine-free pulp,
harvested from managed sustainable forests.

Typeset by Florence Production Ltd in 10 on 12 pt Garamond Book

Printed and bound in Great Britain by Creative Print and
Design (Wales), Ebbw Vale

JEAN MARLOW

Is it really five years since her first books of audition speeches, *Actors'/Actresses' Audition Speeches – for All Ages and Accents* were published? Well the moving finger writes and relentlessly moves on. In these last five years the theatre has kept alive and kicking and Jean has managed to keep her finger on the pulse of a very unpredictable patient. Perhaps one of the most welcome aspects of her work in compiling this latest collection, is her awareness of the nerve jangling process of auditioning for work in a highly competitive profession – and I applaud the success she has had in finding colleagues to give their excellent advice on auditioning and developing new skills to open up more casting opportunities. As well as her invaluable input as co-director of The Actors' Theatre School, she has in the interim played in *The Importance of Being Earnest*, *Romeo and Juliet* and toured in *Pride and Prejudice* in the theatre, worked in films and television and completed another six audition books.

Her latest collection of up-to-the-minute speeches should prove invaluable to the actor seeking new audition material. I wish you every success.

Eamonn Jones
The Actors' Theatre School

CONTENTS

AUDITION SPEECHES

ACKNOWLEDGEMENTS

I would like to say thank you to the actors, directors, playwrights, casting directors, agents and publishers who have kindly contributed to this book.

In particular I would mention Athos Antoniades, Corinne Beaver, Tay Brandon, Frances Cuka, Kevin Daly, April De Angelis, Ellen Dryden, Gillian Diamond, Sue Gibbons, Alison Gorton, John Higgins, James Hogan, Rona Laurie, Jacky Matthews, Katie Mitchell, Hannah Newman, John Quinlan (IT support), Keith Salberg, Carol Schroder, Don Taylor, Drew Rhys Williams. Also Brian Schwartz and Offstage Bookshop, and my editors, Tesni Hollands and Katie Taylor. And not forgetting my co-director, Eamonn Jones of The Actors' Theatre School, and the students themselves who tried out all these speeches for me.

PREFACE

The new millennium has brought some big surprises, not least of all in the world of entertainment where boundaries have been stretched often to unbelievable limits. The 'New Writing Seasons' have thrown up new challenges in theatre, films, television and radio – as have the latest versions, adaptations and revivals of old classics. And every day, more and more is being demanded of actors.

The Peter Hall Company's highly acclaimed production of John Barton's *Tantalus* opened at the Denver Center for the Performing Arts in Denver, Colorado in October 2000. It runs from ten o'clock in the morning until half past ten at night, with intervals, and is described as 'an epic theatre myth for the millennium'. In a cast of twenty-seven British and American actors, and with the use of masks, the eight leading performers play a wide variety of parts throughout this ten hour marathon.

Over here, the Royal National Theatre presented *House and Garden* – two plays performed simultaneously by the same cast in two adjacent auditoria. Yes, you have to be fit to work in the theatre today!

Most of the extracts used in these two new books – one for Men and one for Women – are from recent productions, some of them still running in London at the time of writing. Alan Ayckbourn's very funny *Comic Potential* with its look into the near future of TV soaps when actors have finally been replaced by 'actoids', David Hare's disturbing *Murmuring Judges*, Abdul Khan's *East is East* and Richard Norton-Taylor's *The Colour of Justice*, documenting the controversial Stephen Lawrence trial, all reflect the age we live in and are among many of the up-to-the-minute plays used here. I have also included extracts from film scripts such as *Pulp Fiction*.

All the speeches have been tried and tested by students from The Actors' Theatre School, either in workshops, at auditions, or in the London Academy of Music and Dramatic Art (LAMDA) and Guildhall School of Music and Drama examinations. As far as possible I have avoided using extracts included in other audition books.

I hope these books will fulfil a need for both student and professional actors alike, and also be a reminder of the many good plays seen in London and the provinces – and often too briefly on the 'fringe'.

MORE ABOUT AUDITIONING

You've made up your mind to become an actor. But before you can even begin you're faced with 'competition'. You apply for drama school, but first you have to be selected from what seems like hundreds of other people who all have the same idea. You have to audition. 'Fear of failure' starts to creep up on you. And you have to push it away, otherwise it can 'dog' you all the way through your life as an actor. An audition or 'casting' is not an examination or some sort of test to see who gets the highest grades. It may not seem fair at the time, but very often you just weren't what the auditioner, director or casting director was looking for. You didn't fit the bill.

A friend of mine, not long out of drama school, was touring in a production of *Spring and Port Wine* playing 'Hilda', the daughter of a strict father who is determined to make her eat a herring for dinner which she hates. Throughout the play the herring is put before Hilda at every meal, but she steadfastly refuses to eat it. Then the herring disappears and the family cat is suspected. The cat was played by a large ginger tom called Hughie – that only his owner could love. The show went well, the notices were good, and when a casting director came in on the second week of the tour, the actors had high hopes of getting 'something on television'. To everyone's astonishment the only actor offered a part was Hughie. The casting director was casting a cat food commercial. Suddenly Hughie had become a star and the film company sent a limousine to take him to the studios each day.

Always remember you haven't failed. You simply weren't selected – and in this case the cat got the job!

A musical director, who has sat through hundreds of auditions for West End musicals confirmed this. If someone arrives to audition and they are not what the director has in mind, they will probably be stopped after a few bars of music and sent away with a 'Thank you, we'll let you know.' The next artist to arrive may not be nearly as good, but will often get a recall because he or she looks right for the part.

A director is just as anxious to cast the right person as you are to get the job, particularly if he is putting on a whole season of plays. Does this actor look young enough to play down to seventeen, can this actress age from twenty to forty-five. Are they going to contrast

1

well with the rest of the company who have already been cast? Should we be looking for a 'name'? It is not always the best actor or actress that gets the part. How can it be?

So throw 'failure' and 'rejection' out of your vocabulary. As long as you've done your very best to prepare for your audition, you haven't failed, you've simply added to your experience and may even be called back another time. Only the other day an actor telephoned to say he had just auditioned for a lead in the tour of *Joseph and the Amazing Technicolor Dreamcoat*. The director told him he was wrong for the part, but liked his audition and arranged to see him again for a new show being cast at the end of the month.

But let's have a look at the first audition you are most likely to encounter when you are thinking about 'going into the business' – the drama school audition.

The Drama School Audition

Tim Reynolds, Principal of the Academy Drama School, Whitechapel, has this advice for would be drama students:

'I pondered for some time, wondering what could possibly be added to the advice already given in Jean's earlier books, *Actors'/Actresses' Audition Speeches – for All Ages and Accents*. Then I decided simply to put in writing the advice and help we give to those students who are on our one year Medallion Course – for seventeen to twenty year olds – which is solely dedicated to preparing them to audition for drama school, and for the reality of the three-year course they are hoping to enter.

First. Be very sure of your dedication. Drama schools are not about getting into television soap operas, or block-busting movies. They are more concerned with training your talents to the extent that you can rise to any challenge that may come your way. Although some actors achieve fame and fortune, most do not, and unless you feel sure that working regularly in the profession you love is sufficient reward, think again before you embark on a training you will probably never complete.

Do not undertake to audition for drama school until you feel entirely prepared. Although it is true to say that the people who are auditioning you want to offer you a place, there is enormous competition from other applicants. If you come to your audition with a clear understanding of your speeches and a strong idea of what you want to do with them, that's half the battle. The Academy audition literally hundreds of prospective students each year, so we have a very good idea of what we are looking for. Here are a few tips which may be of help.

Audition for all the drama schools, even the ones that are not on the top of your list. The more auditions you attend the better you get at auditioning and the better your chances. If you decide that there is only one school you could possibly go to, and then don't get in you'll have to wait 'till next year to apply again, and this could go on until you collect your pension. Strike while the iron is hot, and increase your chances. You may get more than one offer, so you could have a choice. If you do, it's important that you go to the one in which you felt most comfortable at your audition.

Find out as much as you can about the school for which you are auditioning. Each school has its own criteria, and to an extent, its own method of training, and it is as well to know as much about that particular school as possible. For example, the Academy is most widely known for being the first full time evening and weekend drama school, training over six terms which are on average twelve weeks in length. This kind of information is available in the various prospectuses, which you should study with great care before your audition.

Look very carefully at the requirements for the audition, and make sure you follow them to the letter. There may well be a workshop. Listen carefully to the instructions given, and if there is anything you do not understand, you must ask. Always be in good time for your audition. Punctuality is essential in the acting business, and this must start with your training. Know your speeches thoroughly. Not just well enough to recall the lines, but so well that you can concentrate entirely on the character you are playing. You are likely to be asked to do the speech in an entirely different way, and time and again I have seen prospective students totally unable to recall the speech under such conditions.

The speeches from this book are chosen with care, but they are only a section of the play. What has your character done or lived through before the speech begins? What will he or she go on to do afterwards. It is vital that you read the whole play, not just because you will be asked questions on it, though you well might, but you yourself will have become familiar with the person you are playing. Every character must start with you, so it is important that you pick someone that you understand, who in other circumstances could be you. Do not choose a character too old, or too young, or whose

3

experience of life is vastly different from yours. The auditioners only need a few lines to know whether you are right for them.

Should you get help with your speeches? Well, yes, I think you should, although some drama schools advise against it. They have seen all too many times the young hopeful before them spouting lines and carefully rehearsed gestures that have been drilled into them by someone whom the procession has passed by, and who would like to live again through you. The right tuition is important. The auditioners want to see your performance and a good tutor will help you realise your performance, rather than give you theirs.

There are one or two drama schools who supply a list of speeches from which to choose. It is not a good idea to do these speeches for other auditions because they are known to the other schools and it might appear that you are simply too lazy to learn another speech.

Finally, it is important to realize that the odds against you getting into any particular drama school of necessity are high, as they are when you have completed your training. The advice you are being given at the beginning of this book should be used to shorten those odds. At the end of the day, though, when you are turned down, remember it is only the decision of that particular school, and only at that particular time. Never lose confidence in yourself or your abilities.

The best of luck. If you've got the will, the heart and the stamina, combined of course with the talent, you'll get there.'

Robert Palmer is Senior Voice Tutor at the Royal Academy of Dramatic Art (RADA) which auditions between 1400 and 1500 students a year for 30 available places. He had this to say about the importance of a clear, audible voice:

'After auditioning for a place at the Royal Academy of Dramatic Art, workshops are held to determine further the technical and interpretive ability of selected candidates, particularly in a class situation.

On this occasion the Voice Department teachers give an individual ear-test where the candidate is required to sing/hum different notes played for them on the piano, sing a song and give a 'cold' reading of a text, also to participate in voice and speech exercises with a class.

During this the teacher is noting details of the actor's voice-quality, vocal range and speech, in particular any specific voice problems.

As these auditions draw in people from all over the world, the expectation has to be, as in any audition, that the actor is clearly audible and distinct – whatever their own particular dialect or accent.

Therefore it is essential that prior to the event the importance of maintaining a good standard of spoken delivery is realised. It is suggested that the regular practice of voice and speech exercises involving breath-support, resonance and articulation are necessary to underpin both classical and modern material used in the audition.'

Working Today in Professional Theatre

Sir Peter Hall created the Royal Shakespeare Company (which he ran from 1960-68) and directed the National Theatre from 1973-88. During that time he opened its new premises on the South Bank. After his repertory season at the Old Vic, he ran the Peter Hall Company in the West End until 1999 and has since opened his highly praised production of John Barton's *Tantalus* at the Denver Center for the Performing Arts in Denver, Colorado - transferring it to the Barbican Theatre, London in 2001. He has this to say about creative work in the theatre:

'Creative work in a theatre has always been done by a company. Here is another paradox. A company does the best work - but good work can also create a company. It may form itself by chance because a collection of actors in a commercial production have worked together in the past. Or it may be stimulated by the playwright's demands or the director's inspiration. It can happen in a matter of days. But the potent theatre company takes longer to develop, as actors grow together, learning each other's working habits, learning indeed how they dislike as much as how they like each other. Making theatre needs everyone to accept that they are dependent on everyone else. The messenger with one line can ruin the leading actor's scene if he does not speak at the right tempo and in the right mood. The wig-mistress who is late for a quick change can wreck the concentration of everyone on stage. Company work recognises dependency. Indeed it celebrates it . . .At the Old Vic with our small company of actors we found that the audiences' traditional responses were still strong: they loved seeing the same actors in different parts; they had an enthusiasm for seeing young talent develop; a feeling that the group had a strong and intimate relationship with it which was growing with every production. The more cohesive the company became, the more it felt capable of an immediate dialogue with its audience, and the more it felt able to arouse an imaginative response. This is the true process of live theatre.'

Developing Extra Skills

More and more demands are being made upon actors today. In the *Equity Job Information News* recently, actors and actresses were wanted for the excellent London Bubble Theatre's production of *Sleeping Beauty*. They had to be able to sing, play a musical instrument and jive. Without these extra skills, however good a performer you might be, there is no sense in even applying for an audition like this.

Jacqueline Leggo, Agent and Personal Manager, submits artistes for theatre, film, television and radio and has clients working, at the time of writing, with the Royal Shakespeare Company, the touring musical of *One Step Beyond*, the West End musical of *Buddy* and television series such as *Nuts and Bolts* (HTV) and *Without Motive* (ITV). She has this to say:

'When arranging interviews it is important to know that the performer is well equipped with contrasting audition speeches. It would be wonderful if we were always given enough time to prepare pieces which could be angled towards a particular job, but quite often an interview will be for the next day. If an artiste has a repertoire of speeches then the likelihood is that one of the pieces will be suitable. It is important to realise there is a great deal of competition for the available jobs and these days, with many musicals providing work, having one or two songs prepared as well, can only help open up opportunities. Any additional skills are certainly worth mentioning on your CV. For example playing a musical instrument, languages, fencing, horse riding – football has been asked for most recently for *Dream Team* – and driving a car is always a useful asset.'

Jean Hornbuckle trained with the Royal Academy of Music. She is an opera and recital singer and coaches singers and actors for musicals:

'Actors are often requested to prepare a song – sometimes a particular style is specified, or it can be a free choice. Many find this daunting and doubt their singing is good enough, although with the help of a teacher, it is probable that they could acquit themselves perfectly adequately.

Musical ability of any sort is a definite advantage as it can open up opportunities for actors in more varied fields, particularly in musicals where small parts involve only a little singing.

Recently, a well known writer on musical affairs wrote an article bemoaning the dreadful standard of singing in West End shows at the moment, and asking where the good singers in this country are. It cannot be denied there is a real need for well trained singers to meet composers' requirements.

A good understanding of the singing voice and a secure technique are absolutely essential for sustaining a career in any type of music from pop and jazz through to serious classical, and only with proper training can the vocal stamina required to sustain a long run in a show be built up.

Prolonged misuse of the singing voice through ignorance of these things can lead to serious vocal problems affecting both singing and speaking voice, and it is worth considering having singing lessons both to learn about correct use of the voice, and also gain confidence to present a song successfully at an audition.'

Barry Grantham, author of *Playing Commedia*, performer, director and teacher specialising in Commedia dell'Arte and other forms of physical theatre, is also well aware of the additional skills expected of actors today:

'There was a time when all you needed was a small selection of modern and classical audition pieces, a good voice (with a 'Queen's English' accent of course), a few funny dialects, and, perhaps even more important than any of these, a good wardrobe; later you might need some talent but at least you knew where to start. Now you don't know where you are – there is a chance for a part in a prestigious production of *Timon of Athens*, but your agent tells you that you must be able to play the saxaphone and drive a motorbike through a burning hoop. You know the '*Mercy*' speech from *Merchant of Venice* but can you act it while juggling five balls?

You cannot be ready for every quirky possibility but you can prepare for some of the things most likely to be demanded of you by today's theatre, where the straight play is a rarity rather than the norm (much of the repertoire of our National Theatre is devoted to musicals and other 'Total Theatre' productions).

First, perhaps, there is a much greater need to equip yourself by training in movement of all kinds: dancing, mime, stage fighting, acrobatics, period dance and styles, movement which indicates status, comedy and eccentric behaviour. It is a good idea too to treat seriously any time spent on preparation for a musical you may be involved in. You may never be or wish to be in a musical but the experience of its multiple demands will be invaluable. Masks are now often called for and there is a very specialized technique required for working in the different types of mask from the epic full masks of Greek theatre to the half-masks of Commedia dell'Arte. Then there is the whole area of improvisation, which in present training tends to concentrate on soul searching, character analysis on the Stanislavsky model – valuable but not of much help in the 'instant impro' so frequently part of today's audition process.

Perhaps surprisingly, if we look for an all embracing technique to provide us with a training that will fit us for these most recent requirements we cannot do better than to call upon that most ancient of disciplines, the Commedia dell'Arte – or more exactly *Commedia* – the shortened version now used to denote all the skills, but not necessarily involving the historic characters of Arlecchino, Colombina, Pantalone and so on. Here we have physical theatre at its most intense. Here is mask work, mime, movement, comedy, timing, audience communication, and instantaneous improvisation. It can incorporate any performing skill: dance, acrobatics, vocal and instrumental music, circus skills, all fitted into a dramatic framework that can be as truthful as anything demanded by the most dedicated followers of the Method (though its affinities are perhaps closer to Brecht and Grotowski). Unfortunately most drama schools give only a peripheral glimpse of Commedia at best, but gradually it is becoming evident that it should form a central element of any actor's training, sharing equal time with that devoted to Shakespeare, the modern masters, and the training approaches of both the Method style and traditional tuition.'

Penny Dyer, dialect coach for *The Blue Room* with Nicole Kidman and Ian Glenn at the Donmar Warehouse and on Broadway, and the film *Elizabeth* with Cate Blanchett and Geoffrey Rush:

'Never use an accent for the accent's sake. It doesn't impress. Only use what is relevant to the character and the rhythms of the writing. Make sure you feel comfortable with the accent, so that it sits in your mouth with the same familiarity as when you wear a favourite coat. This is one very good reason to see a dialect coach. There are quite a few of us now and it pays to have that hour's worth of confidence building. Also, if you have been briefed to speak in a specific accent, but are unsure what that means, ask a dialect expert, we understand the 'lingo'. If you are asked to read a script in an accent, on the spot – so to speak – ask for five minutes preparation time and go elsewhere to do this, so that you can practice aloud, not in your head. Don't use a drama school audition as an 'Accent Show'. They want to hear the potential of your own voice and speech, so only choose to use an accent if you're really 'at home' with it. Try to master a few accents for your repertoire, especially a modern Received Pronunciation (RP). It acts as a physical springboard for all the rest.'

Advice from the Actors

I asked two actors, who have both left drama school within the past five years to give some tips on auditioning and tell us a bit about their own experiences:

Samantha Power trained at the Welsh College of Music and Drama and played 'Cecily' in the Number One Tour of *The Importance of Being Earnest*. On television she has appeared in *City Central*, *Cops* and *Peak Practice* and was 'Sonia' in the BBC Television sitcom *A Prince Among Men*. She also plays 'Lisa' in the film *Low Down* directed by Jamie Thraves.

'Auditions can be quite an intimidating experience, especially in the early stages of your career, but I believe they can often be quite exciting and enjoyable.

When you go up for a television audition you will usually meet the director, casting director and sometimes the producer. You are often required to read from the script so if sight-reading isn't your strong point – Practise!

It is important to find as much information about the role as possible – what the character is like, the general synopsis and style of the piece – all of which will create a clear picture in your mind and help prepare you for the audition. If you haven't had the luxury of being sent a script, make sure you arrive early enough to look through it.

I remember auditioning for a new BBC sitcom just six months out of drama school. I was sent the script in advance and I read it over and over again searching for clues as to what this character was like. I worked on it with the same approach I would any other role. I had the audition and was then recalled to meet the writers and the producer, and to read opposite the well-known lead actor. I was successful. Much later, I was told by one of the writers the reason I got the part was because 'You came into the room and made the character your own!' If you are prepared to work hard you will see the rewards.

If you are required to do a dialect, it is imperative you do it correctly. Any one of the people auditioning you could be from that area, so if you haven't prepared it could turn into a very embarrassing situation!

Always remember, if it doesn't work out the first time, don't be disillusioned. Decisions are based upon several factors. It is not necessarily a reflection on your ability to act!

So think positive. Be patient and Good Luck!'

Matt Plant trained at the Academy Drama School. He recently played 'Algernon' in the Number One Tour of *The Importance of Being Earnest* and 'The Tutor' in *Anger* for BBC Television, directed by David Berry:

'Sometimes one is asked to travel long distances to an audition. This should never deter an actor as it could be 'the crock of gold at the end of the rainbow' and if it's not, you can always turn it down. Either way it can only add to your experience. At least that's what I thought as I walked into the Gaiety Theatre, Ayr in Scotland! I had already travelled all the way up from London by bus, thanks to the unfailing dedication of our beloved rail, had endured the dictates of Mrs Mince's 'Oh yes, all the stars stay here' boarding house, and was prepared for anything.

The audition panel, for it was a panel, wore suits and for a moment I thought perhaps I was being interviewed for Microsoft! 'Sing Happy Birthday', they said. 'What for?' I exclaimed, this being an audition for Terence Rattigan's *Murder in Mind*. I should have known when they asked if I could 'act like a mole' and 'talk like a farmer', and at this point produced a horse's head (papier mâché). It was only later I realised they had been considering me for 'future projects', whatever those projects were, and in actual fact the Rattigan play had already been cast!

The experience did not put me off auditions, or travelling long distances to get to them, although it has given me a strange aversion to horses! Funny that . . .'

Auditioning for Films and Television

Even the most experienced actors will often tell you they have no idea why they got a particular film or television part or, why they didn't. What are film and television directors looking for? I was once told at a screen test, as I fumbled with the script I had just been handed by the casting director and tried to read it, at her request, without my glasses, 'Don't worry – it's really a 'look' they're looking for'!

So I passed this problem over to film and television casting director, **Doreen Jones**, who cast the film *Orphans* for Peter Mullins, the television mini-series *Prime Suspect* and is currently working on *The Vice*:

'First thing to remember is that generally speaking (I can only speak for myself) you wouldn't be at the interview unless the casting director thought you were good. Nowadays with a very short run-up to the start of most film and television, there just isn't time to see the world and their mother. Generally I only suggest a few actors for each part but they will have been whittled down from an enormous list. I usually bring in three or four actors who represent different ways of playing the part.

If possible, try and find out a bit about the project. If it's an adaptation of a book, directors are impressed if you've taken the trouble to read the book – it shows commitment. Engage with the people you're meeting – it's no good leaning back in your seat trying to look cool – it looks as if you aren't interested; lean forward and show enthusiasm for the project – but don't go over the top. You may be asked to read – some actors have a facility for this and some don't. In order to give yourself the maximum chance, either arrive earlier so that you can familiarise yourself with the part or call the casting director the day before and ask if you can come in and pick up the lines or have them faxed to you. Only the churlish will refuse. This means that when you do read, you will be able to make eye contact with whoever is reading with you (usually the poor casting director) and again directors will be impressed that you have taken the trouble. Very often the director will say after just reading once, that was just fine. If you're not happy, ask to have one more go and ask if the director would like it a bit differently. Sometimes I would like an actor to have another go, but it's tricky for a casting director to intervene at this point – it could look as if they are undermining the director.

Occasionally you will be sent a script before a meeting. This is because the director finds it helpful to find out what your 'take' is on the script. So read it properly, not just once but several times so that you can talk intelligently and in depth about the character you have come in for. Make a note of not only the writer's notes and what your character says but also what other characters say about you. Do not, on any account arrive saying you didn't have time to read it properly. If that's the case, you might as well leave then because it's unlikely you'll get the part. If something catastrophic has happened in your personal life, and you genuinely have not been able to read the script, get on to your agent and see if you can be seen later. If you have had the script you should definitely learn the lines, not necessarily to the extent that you can put the script away but enough so that you don't have to constantly refer to it.

There are still some directors around who don't read actors. It may be that they prefer to rely on their 'gut' instinct or that they and the casting director have worked together many times and know each other's taste. In these cases it sometimes helps to talk about parts that you have played (subtly of course!) that may bear some resemblance to the character you have come in for. If you have come in for a character with an accent that is not your normal accent it is a good idea to think of a story to tell which involves you using the accent of that character.

There are lots of 'Chiefs' around these days and sometimes it is necessary when we 'Indians' have made a decision about who we would like to play the part, that we have to refer it upwards. This is when you will be asked back to go on video. So please think about the part you are videoing for. Don't have a late night if you're going to look wrecked the next day and that's not what the part calls for. It will be the first time the executives have seen you and no amount of us saying that you really are only twenty-three even if you're looking forty will convince them that we have made the right decision. You will not only have let yourself down, you will have let down those who had confidence in you as well.

When you don't get the part, try not to take it too personally. Remember that you wouldn't have been in for the interview if the casting director didn't think you were a good actor. More than likely, the decision will have been made on physical grounds i.e. family resemblance or a physical variation within a group so that the audience can distinguish one character from another.'

Auditioning for Voiceovers and Radio Drama

Patricia Leventon, Royal Shakespeare Company actress and former member of the BBC Radio Drama Company:

'Your voice can be your fortune. A good flexible voice coupled with the ability to sight-read is one of the greatest assets an actor can have. The world of commercial voiceovers both on radio and TV can be extremely lucrative. You have to be able to go into a studio, pick up a script, read it, time it and give the exact emphasis required by the advertiser. Often there are a great many words needing all your articulatory skills to fit them into the ten, twenty or thirty seconds of the average commercial.

Radio Drama is another great source of work. Most of the drama schools now enter their students for the Carlton Hobbs Award (named after the great radio actor of the 1940s, '50s and '60s). This competition takes place towards the end of the academic year, i.e. June, and six students are awarded a place with the BBC Radio Drama Company. They provide a talent base and are usually given a six-month contract enabling them to gain experience of the medium and supplying them with the opportunity to work alongside very experienced actors in the field. For these auditions it is advisable for students to work on their pieces in detail with their tutor as much in advance as possible. Choose pieces you feel at home with. The usual contrast of comedy and drama is expected. Also classical and modern. Only use native accents if you want to use a dialect. There are a great many actors around from America, Ireland, Scotland, Wales etc. and it is not sensible to put yourself in competition with the real thing.

If you're fortunate enough to work with BBC Radio then again the ability to pick up a script and 'lift' the part off the page is a 'must'. For an afternoon play or a longer work on Radio 3 you will get a script with sufficient time to study your part. Raising your eyes off the script and making contact with the other actors or looking straight into the microphone to express your inner emotions and thoughts are the beauty of radio work and are very satisfying for the actor. Radio is experiencing a renaissance in this new Millennium. Long may it continue.

The spoken word is important and the recording field is vast. There are numerous Talking Books, Shakespearean CDs, language tapes, children's cassettes, all giving opportunities to the vocally well equipped actor.

If you love a particular book and have an ambition to read it and as far as you know it hasn't been recorded recently it is worthwhile doing a bit of research to find out if any of the publishers who have media departments would be interested. They'll probably want a 'star name' but it is worth a go.

Simple voice exercises keep the voice in trim and these should be done gently every day. Don't lose your original accent as it is useful for television drama, soaps etc. but work at Received Pronunciation for the opportunity to work in classical drama. Keep reading and above all enjoy.'

Carol Schroder LLAM is an Examiner for the London Academy of Music and Dramatic Art (LAMDA) and an experienced teacher of drama and performing arts. She is the author of several textbooks.

'This is an imaginative, exciting and well researched collection of scenes. Whilst using some well known sources there is a wealth of material from new writers representing plays that have been performed in a variety of theatres from the fringe to the West End and other countries.

The scenes offer scope to actors of all ages and experience and will equip them with a range of material that will admirably demonstrate their versatility, either for auditions or examinations. Many are taken from plays written since 1985 and this is an essential criteria of the syllabus requirements for the LAMDA medal examinations.

It is always rewarding to discover new material, especially that which will challenge the actor and give pleasure both in the preparation and the performance.'

A Word About the Speeches

Each of the following speeches has its own introduction, giving the date of the original production – information often required for auditions and drama examinations – a few lines about the play itself, and the scene leading up to the actual speech. Even so, it is important to read the whole play. Not only will you most probably be asked questions such as, 'What happened in the previous scene?' but also the other characters in the play can give you vital information about your character.

At the top left hand corner of each introduction I have, where possible, given the age, or approximate age of the character, and their nationality, and/or the region or area they come from. If a region or nationality is not mentioned then standard English, RP (Received Pronunciation), or your own voice should be used. When a play is in translation, or is set in another country, only characters foreign to that particular country need to use an accent or dialect. The characters in Maxim Gorky's *Summerfolk* would not be speaking in Russian voices any more than those in *Oroonoko* need to use African voices. In other words – use your own voice. No funny accents! Here again, reading the whole play should give you a better idea of whether the character is suited to you.

AUDITION SPEECHES
for MEN

ANDREW BUCHAN
Scots
25-45

THE ABSENCE OF WAR
David Hare

First produced at the Olivier Theatre in 1993 as part of the Royal National Theatre's David Hare trilogy.

After a long period of turmoil, the Leader's office has imposed an uneasy period of calm on the Labour Party. But the Leader, George Jones, knows he has only one chance of power. This is the third part of a trilogy of plays about British institutions and looks at the way politicians think and act today and the problems that beset them.

This early scene is set in front of the Cenotaph Memorial. Big Ben chimes and a gun fires in salute. The two minute silence begins. A few moments and a light picks out ANDREW BUCHAN standing at the side of the ceremony. He wears a thick coat and is described as heavily built, wearing spectacles and passing for any age between 25 and 45 years. He addresses the audience.

Published by Faber & Faber, London

ANDREW

I love this moment. The two minutes' silence. It always moves me, year after year. It gives you a breath, just to question. The questions everyone in politics asks. Why these hours? Why these ridiculous schedules? Up and out of our beds at six every day. Read the papers. When you know already what the papers will say. Grab a quick croissant – a croissant! Jesus, I'm from Paisley – then the first meeting of the day. Seven o'clock and I'm there. And outside that meeting, another meeting, already beating, bulging, pressing against the door. You mind's already on the next one, the one you are already late for, the one which may – God help us – achieve a little bit more than the one you are at now.

What is this for? This madness? To bed at twelve-thirty. After which the phone goes only twice. And once more at three-fifteen. As it happens, a wrong number. But you do not dare turn the thing off.

(The guns fire again. The Prime Minister *steps forward and lays his wreath at the bottom of the memorial.* George *steps forward and lays his beside it. The* Liberal Leader *steps forward and lays his alongside theirs. Then the three men stand a moment, heads bowed.* ANDREW *looks up.)*

I have a theory. People of my age, we did not fight in a war. If you fight in a war, you have some sense of personal worth. So now we seek it by keeping busy. We work and hope we will feel we do good.

CASALIS
French
20s

ALBERT SPEER
David Edgar

First performed in the Lyttleton Theatre at the Royal National Theatre in May 2000 and based on the book *Albert Speer: His Battle with Truth* by Gitta Serena.

Albert Speer was Hitler's architect and Minister of War. Having escaped the death sentence following his trial at Nuremberg, he served twenty years in Spandau gaol. GEORGES CASALIS is prison chaplain at Spandau. A former member of the French Resistance and a man of exceptional humility, he was chosen because he was a Protestant and spoke German. At their first meeting, Speer has asked CASALIS if he believes it possible to become a different man. CASALIS replies that to do so a man must confront the truth of what he was before.

This scene, set in Spandau in 1950 is one of the many talks they have together. Here Speer recalls the time he finally said goodbye to Hitler in the Berlin bunker before going North to try to negotiate surrender with the British. It was in a small room in a Navy barracks that he heard of Hitler's death and felt 'free of him at last'.

Published by Nick Hern Books, London

CASALIS
You felt that you were free of him? At last?. . . Of course. You were
an expert, not a politician. . . . You had sought where possible to
improve the conditions of your workers. . . . You had visited one
concentration camp. . . . You were ignorant of a systematic plan to
murder - . . . But what do you think you would have done, if you
had known? . . .
No, Herr Speer. I don't think you've been lying. But I must tell you
the questions that remain. You have told me you were let down by
this man who had promised you so much. But was it really that? Was
it not rather a playing out of what was there from the beginning? Is
it not the case in truth that the hope was always false because the
choice was always wrong? That there was a straight line from your
building of the new Berlin to the blasting of that tunnel by those
miserable slave-workers in the mountain. That the granite for
Germania was quarried by the inmates of Mauthausen. That the
searchlights which obscured the stomachs of the party bureaucrats
at Nuremberg also blinded you to what was being thought and said
and planned. Herr Speer, you have presented me the story of a man
who was inspired by great ideals and saw those great ideals betrayed.
And yet, I see a man with all the intellectual, yes, and all the moral
strength to have seen through all of this. Surely, when you look back
to the first time when you looked into those eyes, don't you ask
yourself, how in God's name was I taken in by that?

An excerpt (abridged) from *Albert Speer* by David Edgar.
Published by Nick Hern Books, The Glasshouse,
49a Goldhawk Road, London W12 8QP.

YVAN
approx 30/45

ART

Yasmina Reza

Translated by Christopher Hampton

First produced at the Comédie des Champs-Élysées, Paris in 1994 and in this translation at Wyndhams Theatre, London in 1996. The action takes place in the main room of a flat, the scenes unfolding successively at Serge's, YVAN's and Marc's. Nothing changes except the painting on the wall.

Serge has bought a modern painting for a great deal of money. Marc strongly disapproves of the purchase, questioning his friend's obsession for a white canvas with white lines on it. The once valued friendship becomes more and more strained as YVAN tries to placate them both, only succeeding in upsetting himself and making matters even worse.

Published by Faber & Faber, London

YVAN

Oh, shit! What have I ever done to you? Shit!

(He bursts into tears.)

(Time passes.)

It's brutal what you're doing! You could have had your fight after the 12th, but no, you're determined to ruin my wedding, a wedding which is already a catastrophe, which has made me lose half a stone and now you're completely buggering it up! The only two people whose presence guaranteed some spark of satisfaction are determined to destroy one another, just my luck!... *(to Marc)* You think I like packs of filofax paper or rolls of sellotape, you think any normal man wakes up one day desperate to sell expandable document wallets?...What am I supposed to do? I pissed around for forty years, I made you laugh, oh, yes, wonderful, I made all my friends laugh their heads off playing the fool, but come the evening, who was left solitary as a rat? Who crawled back into his hole every evening all on his own? This buffoon, dying of loneliness, who'd switch on anything that talks and who does he find on the answering machine? His mother. His mother. And his mother.

(A short silence.)

...Don't get yourself in such a state? Who got me in this state in the first place? Look at me – I don't have your refined sensibilities. I'm a lightweight. I have no opinions. . . . Don't tell me to calm down! What possible reason do I have to calm down, are you trying to drive me demented, telling me to calm down? Calm down's the worst thing you can say to someone who's lost his calm! I'm not like you, I don't want to be an authority figure, I don't want to be a point of reference, I don't want to be self-sufficient, I just want to be your friend Yvan the joker! Yvan the joker!

(Silence.)

GEORGE IV
50s

BATTLE ROYAL
Nick Stafford

First performed on the Lyttleton stage of the Royal National Theatre in December 1999.

The play follows the events of the tempestuous marriage of GEORGE IV and his outspoken wife, Caroline of Brunswick – from their first disastrous meeting in 1795 prior to the wedding, through their inevitable separation and his failed attempt to divorce her for adultery, through to her death in 1821.

It is 1820. The old King has just died and GEORGE is dreading Caroline's return from Italy, where she has been living at the Villa d'Este. In this scene he is dining with his mistress, Maria Fitzherbert, and his brother William. Colonel McMahon stands by him, feeding him with papers.

Published by Faber & Faber, London

GEORGE

So I said to him, 'Lord Liverpool, how much stoicism would you be able to muster if you were in my position? If your wife had been so ungovernable that to get her out of the way you'd agreed that she should voyage abroad on a fat income, then, when your father died and you inherited - even whilst you mourned your father - you were plagued by speculations that she was planning to return and once again plunge your life into the waters of misery? If you were I, Lord Liverpool - forget that I am King, and set aside that you are Prime Minister' - that sent a shiver down his spine, for he adores being Prime Minister and would hate to be set aside - 'setting aside our stations, if we were the humblest men on earth, we would be forgiven the anxiety occasioned by the possible return of such an errant spouse. As Regent I stoically tolerated her misdemeanours, but as King it is imperative that I and my country are respected and shown due dignity, therefore understand it is necessary that you support me in my desire to be divorced from her.' . . . [He replied] that he would have to consult his peers. So I said that whilst he was doing that I would continue to consult my advisers *vis à vis* my new government. I know that he fears there's plenty of other Tories who'd jump at the chance to usurp him as Prime Minister - . . . But when Colonel McMahon approached - informally - the two leading candidates, both said they couldn't contemplate stepping into Lord Liverpool's shoes in such circumstances. . . . But Colonel McMahon was only sounding out if they'd theoretically step into the Prime Minister's shoes, so of course they said no, in theory, but in practice, if it came to it I've no doubt that they'd usurp him.

ERIC
late 20s/30s

BOUNCERS
1990s Remix
John Godber

First presented by Hull Truck Company at the Assembly Rooms, Edinburgh as part of the Edinburgh Festival Fringe in 1984 and nominated for 'Comedy of the Year'. It was then performed at the Arts Theatre, London in 1986. This new version was presented by Hull Truck in 1991 and yet another updated version opened at the Whitehall Theatre, London in 2001.

Friday night is club night and the Bouncers come alive. The four Bouncers, LUCKY ERIC, Judd, Ralph and Les, portraying over twenty different characters from giggly girls at the hairdressers, to actors in blue videos and lads on the make, invite us to join them in a night on the town.

In this scene, ERIC - as himself - steps forward to talk to the audience.

Published by Josef Weinberger Plays, London

ERIC

I'm sat in this pub, just an ordinary pub, and it's Christmas. Everybody's had one over the eight. And there's a group of lads, football supporters, that type, eleven stone, walking about like they think they're Frank Bruno. And there's this girl nineteen, twenty, and she's drunk, and she's got it all there, the figure, the looks. The lads are laughing, joking with her. 'Give us a kiss eh?' And she does. Well, it's Christmas, I think, well, it is Christmas. I sat watching for an hour. She was well pissed; they all had a go, kissing her, feeling her, lifting her skirt up. Nobody noticed, pub was packed. Merry Christmas they'd say, and line up for another kiss and a feel, each one going further than the other, until I could see the tops of her thighs bare. And in that pub, she had them all, or they had her, six of 'em, in a pub. Nobody noticed, nobody noticed but me. It was a strange feeling, a weird feeling, I remember walking over to where they were. I was aroused more than ever before in my life. I'm so powerful, so powerful. I stood in front of them, looking at them. The first head was quite hard, but the others were soft, like eggs; they hit the wall and smashed. The girl stood up. 'Give us a kiss,' she said, 'Give us a kiss.' 'Go home,' I said, 'Please go home . . .'

HIERONYMOUS BODKIN
middle-aged

THE CLINK
Stephen Jeffreys

First produced by Paines Plough at the Theatre Royal, Plymouth in 1990 and set in and around 'The Clink' - a prison in Southwark, London - towards the end of the reign of Queen Elizabeth the First.
  Elizabeth is old and near to death and cannot be persuaded to name her successor. Conspirators are everywhere. Meanwhile, alternative comedian, Lucius Bodkin has been invited to entertain the Dutch Trade Delegation. He has been warned that this could be a dangerous undertaking. Should he accept the offer? The only one who could have advised him was his father, HIERONYMOUS BODKIN - once a famous fool - but he's been dead for ten years.
  This scene takes place in a graveyard at midnight. Lucius has obtained a magic potion guaranteed to raise the dead. As the clock strikes twelve he empties its contents over his father's grave and stands back waiting for something to happen. A long moment - then HIERONYMOUS' voice is heard.

Published by Nick Hern Books, London

HIERONYMOUS
Over here, son.
  (HIERONYMOUS BODKIN *appears in a strange light. On his shoulder is a large, decapitated hawk. He goes straight into his routine.*)
There's this Spaniard, see, comes to London, thinks he's a real Jack the Lad, walking over London Bridge he passes this doxy - . . . - tits out here somewhere, so Pedro thinks to himself, could be in there, know what I mean, know what I mean - . . . .
No bugger wants my act these days. Don't talk to me about getting bookings, purgatory. No seriously, he turns to her and says: 'Hello darling, what d'you think to me three foot ruff?' And she says -
[You] want advice, [son? You're] at the crossroads of [your] career. . . .

I know, I know, you think I don't know that, I keep in touch. . . . Can't say I like the act myself. But then, my old man didn't like my act either. Kept on trying to teach me his imitation of Henry the Seventh, I said no one's interested in Henry the - . . .

Safe? You want to be funny *and* safe. Christ son, you know what you're asking for, you're asking for the poxy moon. Look. See this. A brand. One of three impressed on my skin by the Queen's gaolers. See this. A dagger wound, second house at the Boar's Head, Blackfriars. Some mad Anabaptist reckoned I was taking the piss out the Old Testament. I could go on. The poignards, the vicious knees in alleyways, the thundermugs emptied in my face. But I made them laugh. Sometimes the bastards hated me, but even while they thrust their rapiers in my gizzard, their teeth would dance a smile to my music. I fulfilled the contract of my profession. Our profession. I made them laugh. Through storm and hurricano, through fire and brimstone, at the moment the battleaxe was whistling towards the neck, I would set the giggling gums in motion. It is your mystery. There are only three pieces of advice I will ever give you: never apologise; never refuse money; and stick to your mystery. Stick to your bloody mystery or you will fall into limbo like a screaming soul. Do you understand? . . . Then I'll be off. Would you like to hear my bird sing before you go? . . . Oh yes. A sweet voice, a little disembodied, but a sweet voice.

(He sings.)
Dost thou know the price of wheat
Oh my fair young lady
Canst thou say how I may eat
Oh my bonny lady?
(HIERONYMOUS begins to fade from view.)
You must make them die. You must make them die laughing.
(He's gone.)

An excerpt (abridged) from *The Clink* by Stephen Jeffreys.
Published by Nick Hern Books, The Glassshouse,
49a Goldhawk Road, London W12 8QP.

LUCIUS BODKIN
20s

THE CLINK
Stephen Jeffreys

First produced by Paines Plough at the Theatre Royal, Plymouth in 1990 and set around 'The Clink' – a prison in Southwark, London – towards the end of the reign of Queen Elizabeth the First.

Elizabeth is old and near to death and cannot be persuaded to name a successor. Conspirators are everywhere. Meanwhile, alternative comedian, LUCIUS BODKIN, determined to hit the big time, has accepted an offer from the Queen's Lady in Waiting to entertain the Dutch Trade Delegation. He has been instructed to include as many jokes about Dutchmen as possible, as the Dutch love to be insulted.

In this scene LUCIUS has just been introduced to the Delegation. At first the Dutch stamp their feet in approval, but as the act progresses it becomes obvious that LUCIUS has been 'set up'. The Dutch become more and more incensed as insult follows insult. Frobisher, the Queen's Chief Privy Councillor steps forward to prevent a stampede and is stabbed to death. LUCIUS finishes his act with the dead body of Frobisher propped up in front of him.

Published by Nick Hern Books, London

LUCIUS
Staying in London long are you? A week, did you say? It's long enough. (*Holds up skull.*) Two days. It's true. He only came over to sign a bill of lading. Last Tuesday it was. Gentleman over there doesn't believe me. No, not you, the one next to you in the big hat. Oh sorry, madam, no offence. Anyway, over here last week, now he looks like this. Prussian feller. Improved him, hasn't it? No, it's this plague we've been getting. Seriously. Lot of it about. They come round and paint a big blue cross on your door. Nice touch that. Woman lives next to me went out and got infected deliberately. She did. I said what you do that for, she said I've been living in this house thirty year and this is the first time that door's seen a lick. (*Pause.*) Thirty year. Never seen a lick. Blue paint. . . .

No, it's a funny place Holland and no mistake. Been there have you? Sorry, course you have. I forget myself from time to time. Talk funny, don't they. Very strange. I was over there last year, I meet this bloke walking down the road, I say: 'Where am I?', he says: 'Utrecht'. I say: 'I know how I bloody got here', he says: 'That's the name of the place.' I say: 'Can you shut your horse up a minute, I can't hear a word you're saying.'

(There is a definite rustle of disapproval. LUCIUS *is bewildered but sticks to his act.)*

No, there's a Frenchman, an Englishman and a Dutchman. They decide to open a tavern. A tavern. They want it to look marvellous, very chic, the latest thing, covers on the seats. The Frenchman says: 'Ah want zeez seatz covered in zee finest French lace.' The Englishman says: 'I want these seats covered in the finest English wool'. The Dutchman says: 'I want these seats covered in arses.' *(Pause.)* Arses.

(A bread roll bounces off his head. He carries on gamely. he gets three oranges out of his jerkin and starts juggling with them.)

No, no, don't knock it, it's difficult this bit. What's even harder is, while you're doing it, you have to think of the names of three famous Dutchmen. . . . William of Orange? No, famous Dutchmen, not famous greengrocers.

(The Dutch *are now in open revolt.* Frobisher *tries to intervene to prevent them storming the stage. Swords are drawn,* Frobisher *is stabbed.)*

. . . Don't blame me. I mean, I was just up here doing my act. It was one of you.

(Nobody is sure what to do, but LUCIUS *has made up his mind to escape.)*

I told you London was dangerous. . . . But no, Ladies and Gentlemen, you really have been a marvellous audience, but we must go now, me, and my mate, another engagement to fulfil. So it's goodnight from me, Lucius Bodkin, and goodnight from him. It's the first time we've ever worked together as a double act, look out for us, we call ourselves, the quick and the dead. That's right, lady, I'm the quick one.

(He manipulates Frobisher's *hand.)*

Bye-bye. Bye-bye.

An excerpt (abridged) from *The Clink* by Stephen Jeffreys.
Published by Nick Hern Books, The Glasshouse,
49a Goldhawk Road, London W12 8QP.

THE CAPTAIN

THE CLINK
Stephen Jeffreys

First produced by Paines Plough at the Theatre Royal, Plymouth in 1990 and set in and around 'The Clink' - a prison in Southwark, London - towards the end of the reign of Elizabeth the First.

Elizabeth is old and near to death and cannot be persuaded to name her successor. Conspirators are everywhere. Alternative comedian, Lucius Bodkin, accepted an offer from the Queen's Lady in Waiting to entertain the Dutch Trade Delegation. His instructions were to include as many jokes against Dutchmen as possible. It was soon obvious that he had been 'set up'. The Dutch stampeded, the Chief Privy Councillor was stabbed and Lucius had to run for his life.

In this scene Lucius has reached an open space near Tyburn. The dawn is breaking and he sees a figure coming towards him through the morning mist. This is the CAPTAIN - a connoisseur of duelling.

Published by Nick Hern Books, London

CAPTAIN

I am, as it were, a connoisseur of the blade. I have fought some forty-three duels myself, seconded several score and have officiated at countless others. If there is to be a duel, word will come to me. And tonight the word 'Gridling' came to me as I sat in the shilling ordinary. Here, see my gear, I carry it everywhere.

(*The* CAPTAIN *shows* Lucius *a large bag.*)

Pistols, poignards, smelling salts, a measure – that's for distances – a handkerchief to drop to signal the start, maces – I love well a duel with maces, for your mace, wielded by a lusty fellow raises a fine and fatal welt – pray God it be maces tonight. Once – it was in the Low Country – I saw a Hollander contest the issue with a Portuguese: both armed with eight-foot axes, both men blindfold and set at forty paces. Lord, the horrid swishing of the blades as they beat around them in the dark! How the spectators skipp'd at their scythings. Two and a half hours were they lock'd in combat before they approach'd within earshot of one another, and all the time whirling their axes like windmills in a hurricano. At the finish, the Portuguese sliced the Dutchman's noddle at the neck, as clean as a butcher hacking off a foot of mutton for his dog. The head flew twenty feet in the air or else I am a Turk, and was caught at full stretch by a fishmonger's apprentice, and he, tucking it under his arm, makes off helter-skelter to his master's shop, with the mob in full pursuit, for they were polite fellows and did not relish the thought of their countryman's brains floating in the next day's bouillabasso. . . . Give me a duel and let the rest of the world go hang on a mendicant's bellycord.

An excerpt (abridged) from *The Clink* by Stephen Jeffreys.
Published by Nick Hern Books, The Glasshouse,
49a Goldhawk Road, London W12 8QP.

AMOS STARKADDER
middle-aged

COLD COMFORT FARM
Paul Doust
Adapted from the novel by Stella Gibbons

First performed at the Watermill Theatre, Newbury, Berkshire in 1991 and set in and around Cold Comfort Farm in Sussex.

Recently orphaned Flora Poste, heroine and narrator in this adaptation, goes to live with her eccentric relatives – the Starkadders – on Cold Comfort Farm. A fashionable young lady from London, she does her best to tidy up the farm and its inhabitants and encourage her relations to lead a better and fuller life. This proves to be a difficult task, as their insane grandmother, Ada Doom, is determined to keep her family around her and insists that none of them shall ever leave the farm. AMOS STARKADDER, the father of the family, is also the local preacher to a strange religious cult known as 'The Quivering Brethren'.

In this scene AMOS climbs into the pulpit at the Meeting Place of the Quivering Brethren. He has a warming-pan, which he brandishes in his hand as he preaches.

Published by Samuel French, London

AMOS

(to the audience)

So – 'ave ye come? Old 'n' young, sick 'n' well, matrons 'n' virgins – to 'ear me tellin' o' the gurt, crimson-lickin' flames o' hell fire? Aye, ye've come. But what good will it do 'ee? Nowt! Not a flicker nor a whisper of a bit o' good. Ye're all damned! Damned! Oh, do ye ever stop to think what that word means? Nay! Well, I'll tell 'ee. It means endless 'orrifyin' torment, wi' your poor sinful bodies stretched out on red 'ot gridirons in the nethermost pit of hell! 'Ee knows, doan't 'ee, 'ow it feels when 'ee burns yer hand in takin' a cakie out o' the overn? Aye. It stings wi' a fearful pain, doan't it? And 'ee do clap a bit o' butter on to take the pain away. Aye – but 'till not be like that in hell. Nay! In hell yer whoal body'll be burnin' and stingin' wi' that unbearable pain! Yer blackened tongues'll be stickin' out of yer mouth, and yer cracked and parchy lips'll try an' scream out for a drop o' water, but no sound woan't come out! Nay! 'Cause yer throat'll be drier nor the sandy desert! And yer eyes'll be beatin' like red-hot globes against their shrivelled lids! And your twisted 'and'll reach out for that merciful butter-pat! Aye, reach out it will, reach out in all its agony. But yer dunnay bother to reach out in hell. Yer dunnay bother to reach out for that butter-pat. For in hell – there be no butter!

MARTIN SOORJOO
(A lawyer)
NEVILLE LAWRENCE
Black Jamaican
early middle-age

THE COLOUR OF JUSTICE
Based on the Transcripts of the Stephen Lawrence Inquiry
Edited by Richard Norton-Taylor

First performed at the Tricycle Theatre in January, 1999 and then transferred to the Victoria Palace, London.

This is the dramatic reconstruction of the hearings which erupted into national outrage when black teenager, Stephen Lawrence was stabbed to death by a gang of white youths, and the police investigation failed to provide sufficient evidence to convict.

In this extract lawyer MARTIN SOORJOO reads the statement made by Stephen's father to the Inquiry, in which NEVILLE LAWRENCE talks about his son and the events leading up to when he first heard the news of his death and his subsequent encounter with the police liaison officers. This extract could also be played as NEVILLE LAWRENCE himself making his statement.

Published by Oberon Books, London

SOORJOO
(*Statement of* NEVILLE LAWRENCE.)
'I was born on 13th March 1942 in Kingston, Jamaica. I came to England in 1960 at the age of 18. When I first came here I lived in Kentish Town which at the time was notorious for teddy boys and things like that. I was available to work as an upholsterer because I had done my apprenticeship and was therefore qualified. Unfortunately, I was not able to get a job. I believe this was because of racism. . . .

'Stephen was born on September 13th 1974 at Greenwich District Hospital. Stephen was very talented at school. His favourite subject was art. One of the things we discovered was that he wanted to be an architect; he was very good at drawing.

'Stephen has never been in trouble. We brought our children up to respect the law. . . .

'On the morning of April 22nd 1993 Stephen came into our bedroom overlooking the road and said 'seeya later'. He asked me if I was okay and I said, 'yes'. He went down and returned upstairs and said: 'Are you sure you are all right, Dad?' I said, 'yes'. Because I was not working I was not feeling all that good about myself. I watched Stephen go down the road with his rucksack over his back. That is the last time I saw him alive.

'10.30 p.m. there was a ring at the door bell. I thought it was Stephen. It was Joey Shepherd. Joey told me that Stephen had been attacked down the road at a bus stop by the Welcome Inn Pub by about six white youths. Doreen called the police who told her that they knew nothing about the incident.

'I was just praying that he was not dead. We just sat there. All sorts of things were going through my mind. They came in the door. I do not remember the exact words they used, but I do remember they said that Stephen was dead, we could phone our relatives or something like that. . . .

'The next day is very cloudy. We still did not know how Stephen had been killed. We were introduced to the two liaison officers, D S Bevan and D C Holden. Holden made a remark about woollen gloves and a hat being found. It was clear she was implying that Stephen was a cat burglar.

'There were incidents where our car tyres were slashed. It made us feel even more threatened.

'We had fears about burying Stephen here because of the situation surrounding his death. In June 1993, we flew out to Jamaica with the body. He is lying beside his grandmother in Clarendon in Jamaica.'

RAJIV MENON
(A lawyer)
DUWAYNE BROOKS
Black
18

THE COLOUR OF JUSTICE
Based on the Transcripts of the Stephen Lawrence Inquiry
Edited by Richard Norton-Taylor

First performed at the Tricycle Theatre in January, 1999 and then transferred to the Victoria Palace, London. This is a dramatic reconstruction of the hearings which erupted into national outrage when black teenager, Stephen Lawrence was stabbed to death by a gang of white youths, and the police investigation failed to provide sufficient evidence to convict.

In this extract lawyer RAJIV MENON reads DUWAYNE BROOKS' statement in which he talks of his friendship with Stephen and the events leading up to his murder. This extract could also be played as DUWAYNE BROOKS himself making his statement.

Published by Oberon Books, London

MENON

(Reads DUWAYNE BROOKS' *statement.)*

Stephen Lawrence was one of my best friends. We met on our first day of secondary school - the Blackheath Bluecoats Church of England School. Both Stephen and I were 18 when Steve was murdered. We saw each other regularly . . .

In the evening we were hurrying to get home as soon as possible. We were just looking for a bus on Well Hall Road. We were attacked by a group of white boys, one of whom shouted, 'What, what nigger?' I can't bear to go into the details . . .

As we were running from the attack, Steve fell to the floor. I stopped on the pavement. I went back and I bent down and looked at him. He was lying by a tree. He was still breathing. He could not speak. I saw his blood running away.

I ran across to the phone box and dialled 999. . . . I was pacing up and down, up and down. I was desperate for the ambulance. It was taking too long. I was frightened by the amount of blood Steve was losing. I saw his life fading away. I didn't know what to do to help him. I was frightened I would do something wrong.

WPC Bethel said, 'How did it start? Did they chase you for nothing?' I said one of them shouted, 'What, what nigger?'

She asked me if I had any weapons on me. She was treating me like she was suspicious of me, not like she wanted to help. If she had asked me of more details of the boys' descriptions or what they were wearing I would have told her. Those would have been sensible questions.

None of the uniformed officers were doing anything for Steve. They just stood there doing nothing.

The ambulance arrived. They carried Steve to the ambulance on a stretcher. His unopened ginger beer can fell from him on to the floor. I picked it up. I took it home and kept it in my room, until one day it exploded. I am told I called the police 'pigs' and used the word 'c. . .t'. I did not. I don't use those words.

I was driven to Plumstead police station. I now know that in their statements the police said I broke a window in the front office. I didn't. I wasn't even in the front office. It just shows they were treating me like a criminal and not like a victim. They kept saying, 'Are you sure they said "What, what nigger?"' I said, 'I'm telling the truth.' A senior officer said, 'You mean you have done nothing to provoke them in any way?' I said, 'No, we were just waiting for a bus.'

ADAM
early 20s

COMIC POTENTIAL
Alan Ayckbourn

First performed at the Stephen Joseph Theatre, Scarborough in 1998 and at the Lyric Theatre, London in 1999, it is set in the foreseeable future when everything has changed except human nature.

The scene takes place in a local television studio where soaps are being made using android actors. ADAM TRAINSMITH, a young writer and nephew of the Company chairman, has just arrived and is watching the action, fascinated by the 'actoids'. He is hoping to study television technique under Chance Chandler, a director he has long admired. Left alone in the studio playing an old Buster Keaton tape belonging to Chance, he hears a laugh behind him. It is the 'actoid' he has just seen playing 'The Nurse' in the current series. She is still plugged in and explains that she is 'live' and has been watching the tape. She thought Buster Keaton was funny especially 'that little look he gave'. ADAM starts to explain to her the art of the 'double take'.

Published by Faber & Faber, London

ADAM

The look? Oh, you mean the take?. . . The double take. You know about double takes?. . . It's a well-known comic device – the double take – or in Keaton's case the quarter take. The demi semi miniscule take. But at the other end of the scale you have someone like – let's see – James Finlayson – Finlayson's a good example. He was famous from the Laurel and Hardy movies. Do you know the –? No? Well, Finlayson would do takes where he literally took off and left the ground. Bold massive takes. Like this.

(*He demonstrates badly. Jacie looks puzzled.*)

Really funny. When he did them. Do you need to stay plugged in? . . . OK, stay sitting down, I'll teach you. Right. Let's see. Imagine you're reading a book, yes?. . . You hear me come into the room . . . You know it's me, so you don't look up at once. What you don't know is that I am covered in mud. I have fallen in a puddle outside the house and I am covered in black slimy mud from head to toe. You look up casually, you see me, register my presence but your book is so interesting you go quickly back to it. You do that . . .

(*Jacie does so.*)

Now, as you look at your book again, the image of me suddenly registers on your brain. You realize what you've seen. You look at me again. Quickly, sharply this time. Amazed.

(*Jacie does so.*)

All right. Let's do the whole thing. You're reading your book. Here I come. Covered in mud.

(ADAM *clumps rather heavily into the room. Jacie glances at him, then back at her book. . . . She does the rest of the take.*)

(*impressed*) Good! Excellent. Your first double take. . . . We'll make a comedian of you yet.

(*They smile at each other. ADAM executes a rather clumsy comic trip.*)

Whoops!

(*Jacie frowns.*)

Next week, the custard pie.

HONEY
mid/late teens

CRESSIDA
Nicholas Wright

First produced by the Almeida Theatre at the Albery in March 2000.

Actor and talent scout, John Shank, is a trainer of boy players in the London theatre of the 1630s. He has foolishly invested in Master Gunnell's theatre, but Gunnell has disappeared and Shank is on the edge of financial ruin. Before he left Gunnell sent him a new boy, Stephen Hammerton, who begged Shank to train him as an actor, but now it seems he will have to be sold. It is late at night and Stephen, together with an older boy, HONEY, has crept through a trapdoor and into the costume store of Master Gunnell's theatre. It appears to be stripped bare, but behind the curtains are some expensive gowns. If they can take these back to Shank he can pay off his debts and Stephen won't have to be sold.

In this scene HONEY has tried on one of the gowns and is smoking a pipe. Stephen has always admired HONEY who is extremely experienced and one of Shank's most talented and successful young players. Stephen asks him to explain about acting. Is it all just 'a matter of standing straight and saying your lines . . .'

('Jhon' is an old theatre dresser at the Globe.)

Published by Nick Hern Books, London

CRESSIDA

HONEY

It's different at different times. . . . When you're young, you're just a
child being clever. Then it changes. . . . When you get older. When
other boys get tall and clumsy. And their voices drop two million
pegs. We don't do that. We hang on. . . . It's like a baby falling down
a well. You've got its foot in your hand and you don't let go. So you're
not one thing exactly. You're half man, half boy. That's when you find
you can really do it. And it's amazing. It's better than beer or wine.
It's better than smoking. It's like flying. It's like finding that wings
have suddenly sprouted from your shoulders. You come on stage and
everything happens the way it's meant to. And nobody in the
audience looks at anyone else. Because you live in a sort of stolen
time that they can't get to. Except through you. And it could disappear at any moment. You're like a soldier on the eve of battle. Every
night could be your last. And everyone wants to be that special
person on that special night. That's my theory. That's why they grab
old Jhon, J, H, O, N, and give him notes for us. It's why they hang
about at the Actors' Door.

(*He puts out the pipe, starts getting out of his dress.*)
I still get letters every day. Not just from men. Everyone thinks I'm
just a boyish bugger. That's not true. I see women as well. They're
even stranger than men are. They ask me to supper and want me to
bring my gown and make-up.

(*He stands, the gown in his arms.*)
Take it.

(Stephen *takes it.* HONEY *gets the other gowns.*)
We'll carry them back to Shanky. He'll pay his debt to the Board and
you'll stay on. Isn't that what you wanted?

An excerpt (abridged) from *Cressida* by Nicholas Wright.
Published by Nick Hern Books, The Glasshouse,
49a Goldhawk Road, London W12 8QP.

32124

SHANK
middle-aged

CRESSIDA
Nicholas Wright

First produced by the Almeida Theatre at the Albery in March 2000 and set in the London theatre of the 1630s.

JOHN SHANK is an actor and a trainer of boy players. Actresses have not yet appeared on the London stage and female roles are performed by ambitious boys. SHANK is deep in debt and anxious to find a talented young player who might reverse his fortunes.

This scene takes place late at night in SHANK's house when the boys have finished their supper. A new boy, Stephen, has just joined them. SHANK warns him that he may have to be sold as they cannot afford to keep him. Stephen asks SHANK if he was ever an apprentice.

Published by Nick Hern Books, London

SHANK

I was kidnapped. 1599, one week to Christmas. Frosty morning. I took a short cut through St. Paul's, came out at Ludgate and there on the corner I spied a shabby gentleman in a tall hat, standing on one leg like a stork. I quickened my pace, didn't look back, and the next I knew, I felt a pair of arms around me and a sack put over my head. He carried me kicking and squealing through a gate, across a yard, up steps, into a large and echoing room, locked the door, took off the sack and that was my first sight of the Blackfriars Theatre. Where you will play when winter comes. That man was Thomas Evans, a disgrace to the Welsh, Master of the Chapel Boys. There I sat, all day, while every hour or so the door flew open and another boy shot in. Twelve in all. You should have heard us. Screaming, shouting, boys boo-hooing. Most of it came to nothing, because the following day their parents arrived and took them back. Every time a mother and father led their howling child across the snow, I'd say to the boy beside me: 'Mine are next.' I couldn't admit that the only creature on earth who minded whether I lived or died was a shabby gentleman with a tall hat. So there you are. We're fellow-spirits.

(*He gets up.*)

By noon there were only two of us left. Myself and a boy called Salamon Pavy. My pal, as the Romanies say. We went to the Globe in the following year. And then he died. . . . Boys died fast in those days.

(*Outside a church clock strikes twelve.*)

Bedtime. Find a place in the loft. I'm locking up.

(*He blows out candles, leaving one alight.*)

An excerpt (abridged) from *Cressida* by Nicholas Wright.
Published by Nick Hern Books, The Glasshouse,
49a Goldhawk Road, London W12 8QP.

HENRY
middle-aged

DISPOSING OF THE BODY
Hugh Whitemore

First presented at the Hampstead Theatre Club, London in 1999.

HENRY PREECE and his wife, Angela have just moved out of London to a cottage in Stoke Amberley. Their nearest neighbours are a married couple of similar age, Joanna and Alexander. When Alexander hears that HENRY is writing a book, he suggests that his wife might do some secretarial work for him. Over the next two months the working relationship between HENRY and JOANNA develops into a passionate affair. Then Angela announces that she is going up to London for the day and fails to return. The police are brought in but are unable to trace her. HENRY is distraught, blaming himself for Angela's disappearance. His sister Kate invites him to stay with her, but he prefers to remain where he is.

In this scene HENRY is talking to Kate about his affair with Joanna – looking back at what now seems to him a sort of madness. She tells him he is not unique and that she herself had a lover for almost eighteen years. He reminds her of the time he said he wished Angela would just disappear – and now she has.

Published by Amber Lane Press, Charlbury, Oxfordshire

HENRY

I keep thinking of what I said to you. . . . We were talking about Angela finding out. I said I couldn't bear the thought of causing her pain. Then I said, 'I wish she'd just disappear.' Well, now she has. . . . I meant what I said. I wanted her out of the way. Out of my life. Without pain or problems or unpleasantness. Now I've got my wish. . . .

(HENRY *is silent for a moment.*)

Do you remember a boy called Alderton? Geoffrey Alderton. . . . We were at school together. Tall boy, ginger hair, lived near the golf course. We often walked home together past that toy shop near the Catholic church. Do you remember it? There was always a model train lay-out in the window: very elaborate, tunnels, stations, bridges, and all those trains rushing round and round on the circular track – goods trains, passenger trains, everything, it was marvellous. . . . One day, Geoffrey went into the shop. He waited until he saw the shopkeeper talking to a customer, then he went into the shop and stole a model engine. It was a Hornby-Dublo 'Schools' class locomotive in Southern Railways green. I can see it now. He just picked it up and walked out. Nobody saw him, nobody came running after him, his parents never asked him where this new toy had come from. He simply got away with it; totally and completely got away with it. From that moment on, I was afraid of him. Not because I was afraid of being blamed or somehow implicated in his crime, but because he'd shown me that you could break the rules and get away with it. I found that very disturbing.

He dropped dead at a Rotary Club lunch. Only forty-eight. Some sort of delayed retribution, perhaps.

ELIS
20s

EASTER
August Strindberg
Translated by Peter Watts

First performed at the Intima Teatern in 1901 and in Katie Mitchell's production for the Royal Shakespeare Company in The Pit at the Barbican in 1995, it is set in the small provincial town of Lund over Easter.

ELIS HEIST is a schoolteacher. At the opening of the play he has just returned home for the Easter holidays. His father is serving a prison sentence for embezzlement and the family are haunted by creditors. His mother refuses to admit that his father is in any way to blame, but ELIS knows that the whole family are responsible as long as there's a debt outstanding. He is particularly obsessed by Lindkvist, their chief creditor, who he fears could one day seize everything in the house.

In this scene, ELIS is talking to his fiancée, Kristina. As he looks out of the window, he sees Lindkvist coming down the street toward them.

Published by Penguin Classics, London

ELIS

(looking out of the window)

Who do you think's coming now?. . . Our creditor – who can seize
all we possess whenever he wants to. Lindkvist, who has moved here
so that he can sit like a spider in his web watching the flies. . . . Look,
he's coming up the street – he's got his evil eyes on this house
already. . . . He looks as if he's gloating to himself because he can see
his prey in the trap. There now, he's counting the steps up to the
gate; he can tell we're at home, because the door's open. . . .Ah, he's
met someone, and he's stopping to talk to them. . . . He's looking this
way, so he's talking about us! . . . He's shaking his stick now! I can
see from his lips what he's saying: 'This,' he declares, 'is a case for
Justice rather than Mercy.' Now he's unbuttoning his overcoat – that's
to show that no one's going to strip the clothes off *his* back. What
can I answer? 'You're quite right sir – take all we have! It belongs to
you!' . . . Now he's laughing. Not such a malicious laugh either. Good
lord, perhaps he isn't so bad after all, even if he does mean to have
his money. If only he'd finish his wretched chattering, and come in
now and get it over. Ah – there goes his stick again – they always
have sticks, these people who are owed money, and goloshes that go
'swish-swish' just like a cane. [He *puts* Kristina's *hand on his heart.*]
Feel how my heart's beating – I can hear it myself – like the throb
of an ocean liner in my ears. There, he's saying 'goodbye' now, thank
God – and there go the goloshes: – swish – swish – like a Lenten
birch-bough. Ah, he has a watch-chain with trinkets on it – so he's
not entirely destitute. They always have cornelian trinkets on their
watch-chains, like bits of dried flesh cut from their neighbour's backs.
Listen, to those goloshes: 'swish – swish – leech – leech – vicious –
vicious – vicious!' Look out! Ah, he's seen me, he's seen me! [*He bows
towards the street.*] He made the first move – he smiled, and waved
his hand, and – [*He sits at the writing-desk, weeping.*] He's gone. .
. . He's gone past – but he'll come back. . . . Let's go out into the sun.

ABDUL KHAN
23

EAST IS EAST
Ayub Khan-Din

First performed at the Birmingham Repertory Studio by the Tamasha Theatre Company, transferred to the Royal Court Upstairs in 1996 and then to the Royal Court Theatre Downstairs in 1997.

The action takes place in Salford in 1970 where the Khan children struggle against their father's insistence on Pakistani tradition, their English mother's policy of peace at any price and their own desire to be part of a modern society. ABDUL KHAN and his younger brother, Tariq, have discovered that their father is arranging a marriage for them both with the two daughters of the wealthy Mr Shah. He hasn't informed his sons of this as he is afraid they might 'do a runner' as their brother Nazir did before them.

In this scene, ABDUL has arrived back late from the pub and is sitting talking to Tariq, who is planning to leave home. Tariq thinks ABDUL should leave with him. They should both 'just go'.

Published by Nick Hern Books, London

ABDUL

Go, and do what, live with Nazir, what happens then? I don't want
to live without a family. . . . How can I not feel responsible for dad,
or me mam for that matter. I suppose you heard about that?. . . He
gave her a fucking good hiding, Auntie Annie came into work and
told me, 'cause she knew me mam wouldn't. So yes I do feel responsible. Tariq. You know it doesn't even bother me about getting
married, I just wanted to be consulted. . . .
You're right, I was pathetic, tonight in the pub with the lads. We were
sat drinking, telling jokes, playing music, telling more jokes. Jokes
about sex, thick Irish men, wog jokes, chink jokes, Paki jokes. And
the biggest joke was me, 'cause I was laughing the hardest. And they
laughed at me because I was laughing. It seemed as if the whole pub
was laughing at me, one giant grinning mouth. I just sat there and
watched them, and I didn't belong, I was crying, crying so hard I
couldn't catch my breath, so I ran and kept on running. When I got
home, me dad was here praying, I watched him Tariq, and it was right,
to be here, to be a part of this place, to belong to something. It's
what I want. I know me dad'll always be a problem, but I can handle
that now, perhaps I might make him change; but I don't want that
out there, it's not who I am, it's as alien to me as me dad's world is
to you.

An excerpt (abridged) from *East is East* by Ayub Khan-Din.
Published by Nick Hern Books, The Glasshouse,
49a Goldhawk Road, London W12 8QP.

TED
29

THE EDITING PROCESS
Meredith Oakes

First performed at the Royal Court Theatre, London in 1994 and set in a London publishing company in the 1990's.

In publicity beware of everyone, especially your friends. Swept by the cold winds of change toward a risky corporate future, the editorial staff of *Footnotes in History* engage in a desperate battle for survival. TED is Assistant Editor with ambitions to become Editor so that he can get more time to write his biography of Guizot. He has also become involved with Tamara Del Fuego, the corporate image consultant, and has been countersigning certain payments on her behalf. Together they were responsible for a tin of oysters being spilt over the computer while they were having sex in the photocopying room – for which Peggy, the editor's secretary, took the blame. Now his own job is on the line.

In this scene he is trying to persuade Eleanor, a newcomer to the company and whose uncle is on the Board, to put in a good word for him.

Published by Oberon Books, London

TED

That's what I told them, there's nothing to accuse me of. All it amounts to is a couple of countersignatures for payments she said were needed. And I believed her. Was I a fool? Tamara carries amazing conviction. Everyone believed Hitler, didn't they. . . . How dare she question my sincerity. Has your uncle spoken about any of this?. . . You ought to try and talk to him about this problem of mine. . . . Remember the row when Peggy resigned. I think it was me who knocked that tin of oysters down. . . . I think I must have brushed them with my sleeve. . . . I'm glad I've told you. I hate the idea of your distrusting me. . . . But they say confessing a weakness enables other people to forgive you, and they like you all the better for it. . . . Now that you don't distrust me any more, will you speak to your uncle? You're the only person who can help me. . . . If I lose this job I'll have to live at home, which spells the end of my manhood. God. The sofa. God. The sticky table mats with pictures of cathedrals. It will all be over in a minute. That's what the doctor used to say when he gave me my jabs. Didn't he understand, it was that minute I was worried about. There I was, a boy, an entire little universe of wellbeing, and in that minute, a terrible sting was going to come and convulse the little universe, and the boy that was left would not be the boy from before. That happy boy would be extinct. . . . People who are lucky are the ones who don't seem to care what happens to them, I'm desperate not to care, if I go on caring whether I make it or not I'll never make it, I'll continue as a blockhead with strained features and a nervous laugh, I'll be humble, I'll say stupid things, I'll think stupid thoughts, my mind will be paralyzed, I'll never finish my biography of Guizot, I'll never be able to move away from home ever again.

(He rocks back and forth with his head in his hands.)

JOHN
early 20s

HAPPY FAMILIES
John Godber

First produced at the West Yorkshire Playhouse in 1992, the action takes place in a house in West Yorkshire between the late sixties and seventies.

On JOHN's graduation day he looks back on his childhood and teenage years, remembering moments of triumph and despair, as he grows further away from a working-class family who find it hard to come to terms with his ambitions to become an actor.

In this scene it is 1975. JOHN's grandmother has been dead nine months and the family are still mourning her loss. His grandfather cannot face being alone and has come to live with them. His mother has suggested that the whole family goes away together for a caravan holiday, but JOHN refuses to go with them. His mother accuses him of not bothering about anyone else but himself.

Published by Samuel French, London

JOHN

You're right, for once. In fact, do you want to know something?. . . I wish you were *all* dead. All of you - . . . - because we'll never be free until we're born from test tubes. And maybe one day you'll understand what I'm on about. . . . I don't want to spend one day in a caravan. Not with you, nor my dad, or the Queen, the Pope or anybody. I couldn't think of anything more horrible than a week in Whitley Bay. And while I'm on my hobby-horse let me tell you for the millionth time that I don't like cheese and egg when it's cooked in the oven, or fry-up, or bacon and tomato dip or tinned bloody ham. All right, Mother? Do you understand? The world is a big place, it's even bigger than this house. . . . And if you lot want to go and sit in a box on Tyneside watching the rain, and playing happy families, and listening to my mother go on and on about the price increases in Marks and Spencer's and how she can't get her curtains to hang straight, then go, go now. And if you fancy walking with him (*he indicates Jack*) to St Mary's lighthouse and back a million times a day talking about what my gran would have thought about it, good for you. But I'm not. I refuse my consent and, no matter what you say, nothing, and I mean nothing, will change my mind. . . . I'll never go on holiday with you again, ever.

JOHN HALL
young/middle-aged

THE HERBAL BED
Peter Whelan

First performed by the Royal Shakespeare Company at The Other Place, Stratford-upon-Avon in 1996 and later at the Barbican Theatre, London. It transferred to the Duchess Theatre in 1997.

The play is based on the events that took place in the summer of 1613, when William Shakespeare's daughter, Susanna, married to JOHN HALL, a respected physician of Stratford, was publicly accused by her husband's apprentice, Jack Lane, of having a sexual liaison with a family friend.

In this early scene, JOHN HALL, who has not been at all satisfied with his apprentice's progress, suggests that the young man should go home for a few days and think about whether he really wants to become a doctor. Susanna remains with them throughout the interview.

Published by Josef Weinberger Plays, London

JOHN

Hester, would you bring Elizabeth for me to say goodbye . . . but don't come till I call.

(*Hester* exits, *Susanna* remains. JOHN *now takes* Jack's *arm and sits by him.*)

I think it best if my wife stays so that she knows what passes between us in a straightforward manner. I think, first, you should stay home at Alveston the days I'm away. . . . While you're home, think about your position. I'll tell you honestly. I don't think medicine suits you . . . no . . . it isn't just the lapses in behaviour . . . though I have to say, if you were in practice it's a weakness that would finish you. And it's not the learning . . . you have a sharp intelligence when you apply it. I think you have an inner contempt for doctoring . . . yes. As a young country gentleman you've lived life at the gallop. And now . . . to have to smirch your hands with the diseases of the low-born, as well as the gentry . . . to show due concern for all . . . and sometimes risk your life for them. To breathe continually the stench of sickness and have to probe into places you'd rather not . . . to examine urine . . . make cures from common weeds . . . scarcely the business of the son of a gentleman! I came from a family not unlike yours and believe me I know to my cost the foregone pleasures. The curb of emotions and easy human fancies bites very hard at first. Unless you're drawn to fighting disease like the hawk to its prey . . . and have no care for anything except that which will cure, then you should stop now and find the right direction for yourself. . . . I'll speak to your father. . . . He'll see the sense of it, I know he will. . . . It's for the best, Master Lane. God be your guide.

ANISH
Indian
20s

INDIAN INK
Tom Stoppard

First performed at the Yvonne Arnaud Theatre, Guildford and transferred to the Aldwych Theatre, London in 1995.

The play is set in two periods – 1930 (in India) and the mid eight-
ies (in India and England) – and takes place against the background
of the emergence of the Indian sub-continent from the grip of the
Empire. Flora Crewe as a young poet goes to India in the thirties as
her doctor advises a warmer climate. She meets Nirad Das, a local
artist who asks if she would like to sit for a portrait. Fifty years later,
the artist's son, ANISH, visits Flora's sister, Mrs Swan, in London, while
her would-be biographer is following a cold trail in India.

In this scene Mrs Swan and ANISH are sitting in the garden with
gin and tonic. Mrs Swan has been looking at a watercolour of Flora
that ANISH has brought with him. ANISH has been looking at a painting Mrs Swan had found in Flora's suitcase. They exchange paintings
– each one being 'returned to its owner'. In this speech, which has
been edited from their dialogue, ANISH explains how he found the
painting in his father's trunk.

Published by Faber & Faber, London

ANISH

Thank you. I was in England when my father died. It was Christmas day. My first Christmas in London, in a house of student bedsits in Ladbroke Grove. An unhappy day. All the other students had gone home to their families, naturally. I was the only one left. No one had invited me. . . .The telephone rang all day. . . . It would stop and then start again. I ignored it. The phone was never for me. But finally I went up and answered it, and it was my uncle calling from Jummapur to say my father was dead. . . . I went home. It was still 'home'. I learned that my father had left me his tin trunk which had always stood at the foot of his bed. There was nothing of value in the trunk that I could see. It was full of paper, letters, certificates, school report cards . . . (*He takes a newspaper clipping from his wallet and gives it to* Mrs Swan.) There was a newspaper cutting, however – a report of a trial of three men accused of conspiring to cause a disturbance at the Empire Day celebrations in Jummapur in 1930. My father's name was there. . . . That is how I know the year. His birthday was in April and Empire Day was in May. . . . This is how I found out. My father never told me. . . . Underneath everything was this painting. A portrait of a woman, nude, but in a composition in the old Rajasthani style. Even more amazing, a European woman. I couldn't imagine who she was or what it meant. I kept it, of course, all these years. Then, a week ago, in the shop window . . . It was like seeing a ghost. Not her ghost; his. It was my father's hand, his work, I had grown up watching him work. I had seen a hundred original Nirad Dases, and here was his work, not once but repeated twenty times over, a special display. *The Collected Letters of Flora Crewe*, and I saw that it was the same woman. . . . She is in a house within a house. The Mughals brought miniature painting from Persia, but Muslim and Hindu art are different. The Muslim artists were realists. But to us Hindus, everything is to be interpreted in the language of symbols. . . . Yes. That is her. Also the flowering vine . . . look where it sheds its leaves and petals, they are falling to the ground. I think my father knew your sister was dying. . . . She is not posing, you see, but resting. . . . This was painted with love.

HOUSMAN
26

THE INVENTION OF LOVE
Tom Stoppard

First produced at the Cottesloe Theatre at the Royal National Theatre, London in 1977, it is both a biography and an imaginary biography of the life of the poet and scholar A. E. HOUSMAN.

At the beginning of the play, HOUSMAN aged seventy-six, stands on the bank of the River Styx watching the approach of the ferryman, Charon. From there on he retraces his life from his early days at Oxford.

HOUSMAN, now aged twenty-six, works as a clerk in the Patent Office. He and his friend Chamberlain have been watching a suburban athletics match. HOUSMAN's friend, Jackson, is running in the quarter mile. Chamberlain comments on HOUSMAN's admiration for Jackson.

That night Jackson, in pyjamas and dressing gown, is reading aloud. HOUSMAN enters with two mugs of cocoa. He is wearing dayclothes. Jackson mentions that perhaps HOUSMAN shouldn't get too involved with Chamberlain – it might be misunderstood at the office. In this extract which has been edited and abridged, HOUSMAN admits his feelings for Jackson.

Published by Faber & Faber, London

HOUSMAN

Theseus and Pirithous. They were kings. They met on the field of battle to fight to the death, but when they saw each other, each was struck in admiration for his adversary, so they became comrades instead and had many adventures together. Theseus was never so happy as when he was with his friend. They weren't sweet on each other. They loved each other, as men loved each other in the heroic age, in virtue, paired together in legend and poetry as the pattern of comradeship, the chivalric ideal of virtue in the ancient world. Virtue! What happened to it? It had a good run – centuries! – it was still virtue in Socrates to admire a beautiful youth, virtue to be beautiful and admired, it was still there, grubbier and a shadow of itself but still there, for my Roman poets who competed for women and boys as fancy took them; virtue in Horace to shed tears of love over Ligurinus on the athletic field. Well, not any more, eh, Mo? Virtue is what women have to lose, the rest is vice. Pollard thinks I'm sweet on you, too, though he hardly knows he thinks it. Will you mind if I go to live somewhere but close by?. . . We'll still be friends, won't we?. . . Of *course* Rosa knew! – of *course* she'd know!. . . Did you really not know even for a minute?. . . You mean if I dressed like the Three Musketeers you'd have suspected?

You're half my life.

We took a picnic down to Hades. There was a dog on the island there, a friendly lost dog and not even wet, a mystery, he jumped into the boat to be rescued. Do you remember the dog? Pollard and I were arguing about English or Latin being best for poetry – the dog was sub-joined: lost dog loves young man – dog young lost man loves, loves lost young man dog, you can't beat Latin: shuffle the words to suit, the endings tell you which loves what, who's young, who's lost, if you can't read Latin go home, you've missed it! You kissed the dog. After that day, everything else seemed futile and ridiculous: the ridiculous idea that one's life was poised on the reading course . . . . . . (*He cries out*) Oh, if only you hadn't said anything! We could have carried on the same!

RANDALL
middle-aged

A JOVIAL CREW
Richard Brome
Adapted by Stephen Jeffreys

First presented in 1641 *A Jovial Crew* was the last play to be performed before the outbreak of the English Civil War. This adaptation was presented by the Royal Shakespeare Company at the Swan Theatre, Stratford-upon-Avon in 1992.

The two daughters of a wealthy landowner, Squire Oldrents, have run off with a crew of beggars, and are joined by their lovers and their father's house steward, Springlove. They are all looking forward to a life of carefree abandon. In this scene, RANDALL, an old retainer in the Squire's household, who has no time for beggars, enters holding up a purse. It contains twenty-five pounds given to him by Springlove to take care of any beggars who might call while he is away. RANDALL is considering the possibility of keeping the money for himself, when the Squire arrives with his friend, Hearty. He asks after Springlove. RANDALL is not sure where he is, but thinks he has gone to measure land. He begs the Squire to take the purse from him. The temptation of carrying all that money about with him is too great.

Published by Josef Weinberger Plays, London

RANDALL

Well, go thy ways, Springlove. If ever any just or charitable steward
was commended, sure he shall be at the last quarter day. Here, in this
bag, is five and twenty pounds for this quarter's beggar charge. And
(if he return not by the end of this quarter) here's order to a friend
to supply for the next. Five and twenty pounds! This is the heaviest
bag I ever toted in my life, and in my youth I was bearer of my Lady
Retford's bonnet-boxes. If I now should turn this money to mine own
use! Ha! Dear devil tempt me not. To rob the poor is a poor trick;
every churchwarden can do't. But something whispers me that my
master for his steward's love will supply the poor however I may
handle the matter. Then I rob the steward if I restore him not the
money at his return. Away temptation, leave me. I am frail flesh; yet
I will fight with thee. But say the steward never return. Oh, but he
will return. Perhaps he may not return. Turn from me, Satan; strive
not to clog my conscience. I would not have this weight upon't for
all thy kingdom. . . .

(*Enter* Oldrents *and* Hearty, *drinking.*)

Of Springlove, sir, I know not. But here is his money. I pray that I be
charged with it no longer. The devil and I have strain'd courtesy these
two hours about it. I would not be corrupted with the trust of more
than is my own. Mr. Steward gave it me, sir, to order it for the beggars.
He has made me steward of the barn and them while he is gone (he
says) a journey to survey and measure lands. Some purchase, I think,
for your worship. . . . No, sir, I beg you sir. I have not had it so many
minutes as I have been in several minds about it, and most of them
dishonest.

TALLBOY
20s

A JOVIAL CREW
Richard Brome
Adapted by Stephen Jeffreys

First presented in 1641, *A Jovial Crew* was the last play to be performed before the outbreak of the English Civil War. This adaptation was presented by the Royal Shakespeare Company at The Swan Theatre, Stratford-upon-Avon in 1992.

The two daughters of wealthy Squire Oldrents, have run off with a crew of beggars and are looking forward to what they imagine to be a life of carefree abandon. They are joined by their lovers and their father's house steward, Springlove. Justice Clack, the local magistrate, has betrothed his ward, Amie, to young TALLBOY, but she has run away with his clerk, Martin, and has also met up with Springlove and the beggars and decided to go along with them.

In this scene TALLBOY and Justice Clack's son, Oliver, arrive outside Squire Oldrents' house. They are carrying riding switches. TALLBOY has just found out that Amie has left him and is pouring out his troubles to Oliver. The Squire's servants bring them drinks and Oliver tries to comfort him, but to no avail. Whenever TALLBOY makes an effort to put Amie out of his mind, he gets upset again and eventually ends up crying.

Published by Josef Weinberger Plays, London

TALLBOY

She's gone. Amie is gone. Ay me, she's gone, and has me left of joy
bereft to make my moan. Oh, me, Amie. . . . Cry! Who cries? Do I cry,
or look with a crying countenance? I scorn it, and scorn to think on
her but in just anger. . . . Nay, it shall hold. And so let her go, for a
scurvy what-d'ee call't. But something of mine goes with her, I am
sure. She has cost me in gloves, ribbons, scarfs, rings, and such like
things, more than I am able to speak of at this time. Oh – . . . I scorn
it again and let her go again, and hang herself, and the rogue that's
with her. I have enough, and am heir of a well known estate, and that
she knows. And therefore, that she should slight me and run away
with a wages-fellow, that is but a petty clerk and a serving man.
There's the vexation of it. Oh, there's the grief and the vexation of
it. Oh – . . . I know not what to drink. What's best for a broken heart
and a frail constitution? . . . I am glad I am rid of her (d'ee see) before
I had more to do with her – . . . For should I have married her before
she had run away (d'ee see), and that she had run away (d'ee see)
after she had been married to me (d'ee see), then I had been a
married man without a wife (d'ee see). Where now, she being run
away before I am married (d'ee see), I am no more married to her
(d'ee see) than she to me (d'ee see). And so long as I am none of
hers (d'ee see) nor she none of mine (d'ee see), I ought to care as
little for her, now she is run away (d'ee see), as if she had stay'd with
me, d'ee see? . . . I perceive it now, and the reason of it; and how, by
consequence (d'ee see) I ought not to look any further after her.
(*Cries*.) But that she should respect a poor base fellow, a clerk at the
most and a serving man at best, before me, that am a rich man at the
worst and a gentleman at least, makes me – (*He cries*.)

ALAN BENNETT 2
middle-aged

THE LADY IN THE VAN
Alan Bennett

First performed at the Queen's Theatre in 1999 and adapted by the author from his autobiographical memoirs, it is the story of Miss Mary Shepherd whom Alan Bennett first came across when she was living in a van parked in the street near his London home. Taking refuge with her van in his garden, originally for three months, she ended up staying for fifteen years.

The part of Alan Bennett is played by two actors. The first Alan Bennett takes part in the action of the play and ALAN BENNETT 2 describes and comments on it.

In this final scene, Miss Shepherd has been found dead in her van and now the van itself is being hoisted up aloft, while council workers remove their hats, gazing up in reverence. The van disappears from view, the stage darkens and Alan Bennett and ALAN BENNETT 2 are on their own.

Published by Faber & Faber, London

ALAN BENNETT 2

Starting out as someone incidental to my life, she remained on the edge of it so long she became not incidental to it at all. As homebound sons and daughters looking after their parents think of it as just marking time before their lives start, so like them I learned there is no such thing as marking time, and that time marks you. In accommodating her and accommodating to her, I find twenty years of my life has gone. This broken-down old woman, her delusions and the slow abridgement of her life with all its vehicular permutations . . . these have been given me to record as others record journeys across Tibet or Patagonia or the thighs of a dozen women. Actually her only permanent legacy is moths . . . or moth, as the upper classes say. Moths, which I thought went out with my childhood, Mr Attlee, utility furniture and Cremola pudding, now infest my home and the houses of all my neighbours, their eggs like a smudge on the fabric, clustered on the edge of the papers that I sift through for this play. . . .

(*He is going off when he breaks back to address the audience.*)
Look. This has been one path through my life . . . me and Miss Shepherd. Just one track. I wrote things; people used to come and stay the night, and of both sexes. What I mean to say is, it's not as if it's the whole picture. Lots of other stuff happened. No end of things. . . .
And that's true. I'm not making it up.

CARL
American
15

MADAME MELVILLE
Richard Nelson

First performed at the Vaudeville Theatre, London in October 2000, it is set in Paris in 1966.

Madame Melville is the story of CARL, a fifteen year old American boy and his brief relationship with his literature teacher, the beautiful Claudie Melville. Claudie invites CARL to join her special students who meet twice a week to see and discuss the latest films. The discussions take place in her apartment over chocolates and cocoa or tea. One evening she persuades him to stay on after the others have left. He misses his last train and she suggests he spends the night with her. She promises to take him to the Louvre the following afternoon.

In this speech, CARL describes to the audience, their walk along the Quai du Louvre and Claudie's meeting up with his mathematics teacher, Monsieur Darc.

Published by Faber & Faber, London

CARL

Outside we walked together along the Quai du Louvre. Mme Melville stopped at a kiosk and purchased a small book of paintings from the museum. I watched her take out her money, bending a leg to hold up the purse. The late-afternoon, early summer's sun seemed to touch her and set her apart from the world. As if a sculpture. As if a work of art.

(*Beat.*)

I felt more desire than I'd ever in my life felt before.

(*Beat.*)

The book was for me. She brushed back her hair, which the wind off the Seine kept blowing across her face. 'A souvenir,' she explained, as she placed it into my jacket pocket. The expression on my face, I think, stopped her, stopped her smiling. And then for the first time, though we had been together all day, all night, in her apartment, in her bed, I reached and I touched her. I touched her arm, and then held it. And I would have kissed her – until then I had never kissed a girl – but I would have kissed her had she not suddenly run off.

(*Short pause.*)

She ran to a man I recognised as Monsieur Darc, my mathematics teacher at school. With him was his young daughter holding a balloon. They kissed each other on the cheeks. They spoke. She seemed to talk very sternly at him. They did not kiss good-bye.

(*Beat.*)

Walking home she asked if I wanted to stop for coffee. Then she ordered wine. Suddenly it was like I wasn't even there. she found a pair of sunglasses in her bag and put them on. We sat there for a long time. And then we returned to her apartment.

BARRY
London
35

MURMURING JUDGES
David Hare

First performed in the Olivier Theatre at the Royal National Theatre, London in 1991 and revived as part of the David Hare trilogy in 1993. The title of the play is from a legal expression meaning to 'speak ill of the judiciary', which is still an offence in Scottish Law.

The play centres around a young lawyer's first case and takes us through the criminal justice system – involving the police, the courts and the prisons – a system which is cracking at the seams.

BARRY HOPPER is the detective constable responsible for the arrest of three young men. There is some doubt about the involvement of the third, Gerard McKinnon, who has been sent down for five years. BARRY's colleague and girlfriend, PC Sandra Bingham, is uneasy about the case. At the scene of the arrest BARRY had sent McKinnon away and had talked alone with the other two whom he already knew. He later lied about this in court. She is not prepared to pretend nothing's wrong. She has to know why.

Published by Faber & Faber, London

BARRY
You know, when I was a kid, I used to go to the pictures. Nearly every week there was usually this guy. He was the hero. Why was he the hero? Because he was the one who said no . . . (*He looks up to check she recognizes this.*) Remember? He always had this kind of certainty. There was always some scandal, or some sort of scam going on. And this bloke'd get up and he'd say, 'I don't care what any of you think of me, but I have to tell you: I think this is wrong.' And all the others would look kind of shifty, and he'd say, 'I don't care, I don't care what you think. OK, I'm out on my own. But there's something more important than any of us. Yes, you see, there's a *principle* here . . .' (*He smiles.*) And I used to think, now why exactly am I meant to like this geezer? I know I'm meant to say, 'Wow what a guy!' But I don't.

(*He turns now and looks at* Sandra, *sure of his point.*) And *you* don't actually, Sandra, all your instincts are exactly like mine . . . . . . I mean I didn't like him. It's all so easy. 'Let me show you my conscience . . .' That's the easy way. The hard way's the other one, the one that's taken by all the poor bloody foot soldiers, like Lester and Jimmy and Dave . . . (*He gestures off stage.*) Who'd never even think of betraying their pals. But they have a talent which no one seems to value. Their talent is for turning up every day. (*He nods.*) Yeah. For being there. And, OK, there's a lot of moaning, they moan in the canteen, they whinge, they complain about the job. But they keep on doing it. And all the shit is landed in their laps. And nobody thanks them. No, on the contrary, it's all directives, it's supervision, it's behavioural correction courses, it's 'Did I hear you make a sexist remark . . .?' (*He gets up, acting out the questions.*) It's 'Are you racist? Are you foul-mouthed? Do you never lose your temper? Do you censor your speech?' Do you put up with all this, all day, day in, day out? Being treated on sufferance? Being scapegoats for everything that goes wrong. 'Oh, there's a traffic jam. There's a drug epidemic. Crime's on the increase. The young have no respect any more. We're not free to demonstrate. We're not allowed to strike.' (*He stops.*) '*I didn't win the pools last week.*' (*He turns savagely towards her.*) 'Hey, wait a moment, tell you what . . . *let's blame the police . . .*' . . .

(*But* Sandra *is not giving way.*)

No. No, I'm not saying that we're all beyond criticism. I'm saying, you stand there, Sandra, you tell stories about how we're all getting touchy. *Touchy?* Really? You're *touchy?* When people say everything's your fault? I can't think why. Surely you can take twenty-four-hour round-the-clock criticism and learn not to react? (*He stops, suddenly quietening to make his point.*) Well, actually you can. By dissembling. That's how you do it. By being secret. By doing things your way. (*He smiles.*) Yes, a copper is allowed something. It's all he's got. You're allowed a few private moments with criminals. You're allowed a way of doing things which is actually your own.

JIMMY
late 20s

MURMURING JUDGES
David Hare

First performed in the Olivier Theatre at the Royal National Theatre, London in 1991 and revived as part of the David Hare trilogy in 1993. The title of the play is from a legal expression meaning 'to speak ill of the judiciary', which is still an offence in Scottish Law.

The play centres around a young lawyer's first case and takes us through the criminal justice system – involving the police, the courts and the prisons – a system which is cracking at the seams. ABDUL KHAN, known as JIMMY, is a plain-clothes man – described as small and spry and a snappy dresser.

This scene is set in the charge room of a large Inner-London police station late at night, with coppers working on papers in the dim electric light. JIMMY steps forward to address the audience, papers in hand.

Published by Faber & Faber, London

JIMMY

Already, you know, you can see the ones you fancy. It gets to be obvious after a while. I can throw my eyes down a crime sheet, and pick the ones where I'll get a result. (*He holds up the list to show the audience.*) There's maybe thirty-five cases. Most of them you haven't got a chance. Like burglaries, muggings, forget it, unless someone caught them red-handed. Which, if they did, it sure wasn't us. An officer on the beat witnesses, actually witnesses, one crime every ten years. Then maybe the case you choose isn't moving very quickly. What happens? Some pen-pusher comes down from upstairs, says, look, the local press are on to us, we need a nice graph. And please bear in mind, it's kind of important, visually speaking, a clear-up graph is meant to go up. (*He relaxes, enjoying himself.*) So you go down the club, you pull in seven kids. You do them for possession, let them off with a caution, and everything's fine. Seven crimes, seven clear-ups. Oh yes, they all count. And everyone's happy with cautions. None of that senseless ferrying, none of those expensive appearances in court. It's public relations. We know that. So does everyone. Except for the public, of course. But public relations is always a bit of a toupee. If you can tell what it is, then it's not any good.

TONY
29

NOT A GAME FOR BOYS
Simon Block

First presented at the Royal Court Upstairs in 1995.

Once a week three cabbies, TONY, Oscar and Eric, meet up at their local table-tennis club. Tonight is an important match and they must either win or face relegation to Division Two. This is a matter of life or death – not a game for boys. But can the team survive the pressures from outside on its individual members.

TONY is number one to play, but tonight he is late. When he arrives he has a plaster on his nose, and his main concern is to phone his girlfriend, Lisa, who wants him home. Here he is talking to Eric, explaining the situation with Lisa and recounting the terrible day he's had at work ending up with getting hit by a bucket.

Published by Nick Hern Books, London

TONY

Just spoke to Lisa. If I don't go home like *now*, I'm in big trouble. . . . I told her it's an important match. That I can't let the team down. She hung up. Shit, Ozzie, that's blackmail, isn't it? Once you give in to that kind of thing they've got you, haven't they? . . . She wants me to jack in table tennis and work evenings. . . . She wants us to make more money. . . . To move somewhere bigger and start a family. That's why she wanted me home tonight. I'm dead certain she wanted to tell me . . . you know . . . she's . . . fuck, I can't even bring myself to say it. . . .

(*Pause.*)

Shit, Oscar, I'm only twenty-nine and three-quarters. I'm not ready to start a family. . . .

(*Pause.*)

I'm mini-cabbing weekdays. Weekends I'm on the moped with the 'Knowledge'. And now she wants evenings an' all? She's pushing me too hard, Oz. Too hard, too fast. . . .

(*Pause*.)

What happened with the bucket. Fuck. This is what I'm talking about. This is what she doesn't understand. (*Pause*) I'm about to go to work this morning. I remind Lisa I'll be late. I've got this match, I'll be late. She says she doesn't know about any match, and she wants me home this evening. She's got something she wants to sort out. I say, I've got this very important match. She says if I don't come home to talk tonight she's, right. That's it. She's had it. I say about my team loyalty. That I cannot. That I *will* not let my team-mates down at such short notice. She says she's not interested in my team loyalty. *She's* my team. Where's my team loyalty to her? . . . She was making my sarnies. . . . I take the sarnies and go to work. I'm super fucking tense. (*Pause*) I'm on Cricklewood Broadway heading down Shoot up Hill for the first punter of the day. . . . So I'm stuck at the lights where Cricklewood Lane crosses into Walm Lane. From nowhere this kid with a bucket and squeezy starts jumping all over the windscreen. Now. There's Lisa. The fucking traffic. *I'm in no mood to have my windscreen washed*. . . . I'm just not in the mood. So I say 'No'. . . . I start doing my wipers. The light goes green. I'm holding everything up. The whole world's fucking honking me. The kid - get this, Ozzie - this little kid grabs my wiper, and snaps it off. . . . I'm out of the car in an instant saying, you know yelling - '*What the fuck did you do that for?*' And he comes back, "*Cos I'm having a hard fucking day and wankers like you don't make it any easier*', and . . . (*Pause*) Shit. (*Pause*) He whacks me in the face with the bucket. (*Pause*) Then he scarpers. . . .

(*Pause*.)

A nine year old. (*Pause*) New wiper set me back fifteen quid.

An excerpt (abridged) from *Not a Game for Boys* by Simon Block.
Published by Nick Hern Books, The Glasshouse,
49a Goldhawk Road, London W12 8QP.

AKOGUN
African
middle-aged

OROONOKO
Aphra Behn
A new adaptation by 'Biyi Bandele

This new adaptation of Aphra Behn's novella was first performed by the Royal Shakespeare Company at The Other Place, Stratford-upon-Avon in 1999.

It tells the story of a young African Prince, Oroonoko, who is tricked into slavery, separated from his love, the Princess Imoinda, and transported to the British colony of Surinam in South America, where he is persuaded to lead a slave revolt.

This early scene is set in a military camp on the outskirts of the West African Kingdom of Coramantien. Oroonoko is busy re-stringing his bow when his friends Aboan and Laye enter with other young conscripts carrying drums. They run over to Oroonoko, drag him to his feet and insist that he plays the game 'Old Sage You Danced' with them. While Oroonoko is carried away with his performance as 'Old Sage' the AKOGUN, Generalissimo and Head of the Kingdom's Armed Forces appears. The conscripts have already spotted the AKOGUN and quickly retreat, leaving Oroonoko still dancing. The AKOGUN watches him with bemused interest and then barks out his name.

Published by Amber Lane Press, Charlbury, Oxfordshire

AKOGUN
(*barks*) Oroonoko! ...
What exactly do you
Think you're doing.
Oroonoko? ...
I see. Remind me. Oroonoko,
What were you meant to be doing
Out here in the Forest of Demons? ...
Training to be what? ...
Training to be a warrior.

That's right. This is a military
Training ground, not a playground
For court jesters. Oroonoko . . .
It wasn't your idea. 'They'
Forced you. You disappoint me,
Oroonoko. Let me remind you of
The story of the five fingers – . . .
The first finger said: I'm hungry.
The second finger said: I'm broke.
The third finger said: Let's steal some mangoes.
The fourth finger said: And if the farmer catches us?
The fifth finger said: Go and steal: I'll stand apart.
That is the story of the five fingers. Oroonoko . . .
Each finger had a choice.
Each finger made a choice. . . .
Nobody forces you to do a thing.
You are a prince, Oroonoko.
The heir apparent to the throne
Of our land, a king-in-waiting.
You have already proved your
Bravery in war. . . .
But to be a leader,
It is not enough to excel as a
Warrior. That, and more is required:
To be a leader, you have to lead,
And leadership means taking responsibility.
It was bad enough that you
Took part in that childish game.
That was the least of it. But to try
And evade responsibility. . . .
There's nothing to forgive.
But do remember this,
My king-in-the-making:
'I entered but took nothing.'
Will not save the thief.
   (*He hands [a] bow to* Oroonoko.)
Hurry up with that bow, warrior. . . .
The War Council has decided,
We are going to war.
   (*Exit the* AKOGUN.)

OROMBO
African

OROONOKO
Aphra Behn
A new adaptation by 'Biyi Bandele

This new adaptation of Aphra Behn's novella was first performed by the Royal Shakespeare Company at The Other Place, Stratford-upon-Avon in 1999.

It tells the story of a young African Prince, Oroonoko, who is tricked into slavery, separated from his love, the Princess Imoinda, and transported to the British Colony of Surinam in South America, where he is persuaded to lead a slave revolt.

This scene takes place at the port, where a group of slaves are shackled together. OROMBO, the King's Chief Adviser enters with Captain Green, an Englishman. Green examines the slaves one by one as OROMBO extols their virtues, explaining that he has the exclusive licence to administer the Royal supply of slaves and picks out only the best. Throughout this speech it seems he is never able to remember Green's name, continually referring to him as 'Brown'.

Published by Amber Lane Press, Charlbury, Oxfordshire

OROMBO
Don't thank me until you've
Finished examining them. . . .
The King's own personal collection.
Where else do you imagine they come
From, my dear Captain Brown?. . .
Green. The name is Green. . . .
Of course it is. Of course it is.
You very well know, my good friend, that
I deal only in the very best cargo.
No runny-nosed, sore-infested wretches from me.
No diseased items, no lazy, malnourished
Shipments. I bring you, my good friend,

Only the best. You see, I have done the King
Many a favour over the years.
I scratch your back –
– You scratch mine.
I am that sort of man.
His Highness has rewarded
My enduring loyalty by granting me exclusive
Licence to administer the royal supply of slaves.
That means I sell them on his behalf:
I do all the work, he takes ninety
Percent of the proceeds –
And why shouldn't he? I am by
Definition his slave as well –
And everybody's happy. Except of course
For the slaves themselves.

This supply came in
Only this morning. The King's
Grandson, a brave man –
May the gods make a lesson of him.
Or surely I'm finished –
Commander-in-Chief of our brave warriors –
Took them captive from the theatre
Of war. They hail from a race of
Fierce warriors and hunters –
You
Can see that from their torsos
– From
The interior. They are hard workers
And in great demand. In normal
Times they would be kept in
The palace and trained to be attendants,
Guards – that sort of thing. But these are
Not normal times. Times are hard,
The King's coffers are not what they
Used to be, and – my dear Captain
Brown –
Green.
– My good friend,
One is used to a certain standard
Of living.

LEO KATZ
American
30s

PENTECOST
David Edgar

First performed at The Other Place, Stratford-upon-Avon in 1994 and in London at the Young Vic in 1995. Described as the first serious response in the British Theatre to the tragedy of Sarajevo and a political parable, this play takes place in an unnamed South-Eastern European country.

Gabriella Pecs, art curator of the National Museum, has discovered a partly exposed painting on the wall of an abandoned church. The painting is similar to that of Giotto's *Lamentation* in the Arena Chapel, Padua and could be not only of great value, but might possibly change the history of Western art. Gabriella wants to remove the painting to the museum for safe-keeping and English art historian, Oliver Davenport agrees to help her. Their activities are questioned by the Minister for Conservation of National Monuments and then by American art historian, LEO KATZ who has been brought in as an expert witness. Eventually they are ordered to abandon their work, but before they can leave the church they are taken hostage by a group of refugees who demand citizenship and work permits in exchange for their release.

In this earlier scene, LEO puts the case against the removal of the painting to the presiding Magistrate, Anna Jedlikova, questioning the motives of Italian and German sponsors, Peruzzi and Deutschelectronic who are, according to Oliver, backing the project.

Published by Nick Hern Books, London

LEO

OK. It's simple. What this operation does is to make the painting mobile. And sure, right now, it's only booked in for one trip. But does anybody really reckon that'd be the end of it?

(LEO *gestures round the equipment.*)

You really think, Peruzzi and Deutschelectronic, after all of this, would transport you to the National Museum, assist you with the heavy lifting, and then slope off home?

(Gabriella *did.*)

Come on. It'd be – hey, we got the big bang here, you can't keep it to yourself, what say we take it on a little tour? Just think of all that currency. Or rather, while you guys are sorting out security, maybe more like an extended loan? Or even, now we come to think of it, wouldn't it be actually much happier, and much more accessible to doctors and professors and their ilk, in a nice new hi-tech California gallery with state-of-the-art air conditioning and three gold trowels from Architecture Quarterly? Hey, come on, Olly, wasn't that the deal?. . .

(Gabriella *is appalled.*)

'Cos that's what happens, Gabriella. That's what paintings are. They're stars, of the Hollywood variety. With tours. And fans. And franchised merchandise. And – entourage. And as such, they are, they must be, universal and eternal. Not allowed to change. Most surely, not allowed to fade. To crumble, or grow old. And of course, they'll never die.

(*Slight pause.*)

But paintings do grow old. Their history is written on their faces, just like it is on ours. And like the history of people, or of peoples, either you acknowledge it, and try to understand it, or you say it never happened, nothing's changed, and you end up doing it again.

(LEO *looks directly at* Jedlikova.)

Hey, do you know, there were names here on the wall, from when it was a torture chamber, which they scraped away?

An excerpt (abridged) from *Pentecost* by David Edgar.
Published by Nick Hern Books, The Glasshouse,
49a Goldhawk Road, London W12 8QP.

BRENDAN
Scots/Glaswegian
20s/30s

PERFECT DAYS
Liz Lochart

First performed at the Traverse Theatre, Edinburgh in 1998 and revived at the Hampstead Theatre, London in 1999.

Barbs Marshall is a celebrity hairdresser working in Glasgow. She has her own show on local television and lives in a trendy apartment that she has designed herself. She is successful, but it is not enough. BRENDAN is Barb's best friend and works for her in her salon, 'Razor City'. It is Barb's birthday, but nobody at the salon remembered.

In this scene set in Barb's flat, BRENDAN has called round after work with two hastily purchased birthday presents. The pair of them have just demolished a Chinese meal and their first bottle of champagne. BRENDAN is sending Barbs up about her behaviour in the salon that day, particularly to the shampoo girl, because they'd all forgotten her birthday.

Published by Nick Hern Books, London

BRENDAN

. . . So she's only the wee shampoo lassie and sweeper upper, right?
Sixteen and seldom been shagged . . . Nice enough wee lassie . . . –
Nice wee lassie wee Kimberly! Poor wee Kimberly, the Sowell, Whit
does she know? Nothing.
So she's well into it. Giving it that. And we haven't the heart, huv we,
to go Heard It Heard It? We're like dead polite. We're like all agog. As
if. She's like: 'the shampoo girl's just rinsed off the conditioner at the
backwash when she sees the guys hauns gaun like that, right? Under
his robe. Hits him a clatter roon the back of the heid with the
shampoo spray, lays him oot cold, and here it turns oot –'
You swan in and go: 'He was only polishing his glasses!' . . .
You go: 'Kimberly. Kindly, before you come out with all this keech
from your day-release classes, before you bore your colleagues with
jejeune reruns of ancient urban myths concerning Panda cars, cats
with internal injuries keeling over and snuffing it after eating
innocent dinner party leftovers, or women dying of heart attacks
when they see the dog devouring the turkey giblets their son has
stuffed down their drunken husband's flies – *kindly* check with us,
Kimberly, you goes, whether we've heard this one before, eh? You
will probably find the answer is: Many Times. Many, many times.
Right?'
You go: 'I – for one – have got an eight-thirty. Has nobody *else* around
here got work to go to?' And off you go. El Boss Barbara 'Claus' Barbie
wi your face like fizz.
We're like that.
Wee Kimberly's like . . . ooyah! Pure scarlet.
I'm like: I wonder who shat in her handbag?. . .
I mean, Barbs, give us a break, if you don't even give us a clue how
are we supposed to mind it's your birthday?

An excerpt (abridged) from *Perfect Days* by Liz Lochhart.
Published by Nick Hern Books, The Glasshouse,
49a Goldhawk Road, London W12 8QP.

GRANT
Scots/Glaswegian
26

PERFECT DAYS
Liz Lochhart

First performed at the Traverse Theatre, Edinburgh in 1998 and
revived at the Hampstead Theatre, London in 1999.

Barbs Marshall is a celebrity hairdresser working in Glasgow. She
has her own show on local television and lives in a trendy apartment
that she has designed herself. She is successful, but it is not enough.
She is separated from her husband who has found himself a new
girlfriend, and is approaching her thirty-ninth birthday.

Now she has met GRANT STEEL, an attractive stranger, and invites
him up to her flat. She explains that she wasn't trying to pick him
up, but that his natural mother is her best friend, Alice, and she wants
to talk to him about her. She knows that GRANT was an adopted
child and has only just found Alice, but has decided he doesn't want
to see her any more. She tells him that Alice is heartbroken and tries
to persuade him to let her down gently. Let things cool off naturally.
She asks why it took so long for him to get in touch with her.

Published by Nick Hern Books, London

GRANT

I don't know . . . I . . . wanted to know. (*Beat.*) Did you know my father? . . .

They tell me he was a right evil bastard. . . .

Stabbed to death in a prison brawl in Barlinnie in 1981. That is quite a thing to find out about your biological parent. . . .

Listen, Barbara . . . I've got a Mum and Dad.

I always knew I had been adopted. 'We chose you because we loved you.' All that.

I didn't say anything to them about looking for my natural parents. I don't know why. I didn't know if I'd get anywhere anyway . . .

Finding Alice, well, it was curiosity. A curiosity satisfied.

And I *liked* her. You couldn't not. I mean, I think my own mother would like her actually . . .

But when I told my Mum about tracking down Alice . . . Well, I felt disloyal, that's what I felt . . . . . .

I'd like to . . . keep in touch. . . .

Take all this . . . extended family stuff. I can't handle it. Well, Alice has a husband. Fair enough. Great. And daughters. They are my half sisters. By blood anyway. But what I felt about them . . . well they're lovely girls, yeah, but I didn't feel as if I could feel what I felt I was expected to feel.

Which made me feel really shitty.

It was . . . too much . . .

What got to me was this business of Noelene's Eighteenth Birthday party. *I* don't want to go. Noelene certainly doesn't want me to go . . .

So I thought . . . as I am leaving anyway, soon, – I told you I am planning on going to Australia, New Zealand, Japan – . . .

She wants me to be her son. You see the big problem is: to Alice I'm her son. But to me she's not my mother.

An excerpt (abridged) from *Perfect Days* by Liz Lochhart.
Published by Nick Hern Books, The Glasshouse,
49a Goldhawk Road, London W12 8QP.

SAMMY
20s

A PLACE AT THE TABLE
Simon Block

First performed at the Bush Theatre, London in February 2000.

The action takes place in a Board/Conference Room of a small television production company, where ideals and artistic integrity are quickly elbowed for success and a 'place at the table'.

Adam, a new young writer, has been discovered by script editor, Sarah Slater. This is his first meeting with her and so far things are not progressing too well. Sarah has already been interrupted by two disturbing phone calls and when SAMMY, the runner, comes in with a plate of chocolate biscuits, Sarah excuses herself saying she won't be a minute. SAMMY explains that Sarah has just taken a phone call from Kate, the ex Head of Development who recently lost her job with the company. He advises Adam to leave while he has the chance, warning him that although Sarah says she loves his writing, she only really loves what she believes his writing can do for her.

Published by Nick Hern Books, London

SAMMY
Out there is medieval, Adam. An industry built on fiefdom. Serfs and Lords. Kate was Sarah's, so when Kate was lanced, Sarah became a serf in need of patronage. She now has to prove to James she's worth keeping, 'cause he's made his name travelling light through the business. It's partly what made him so attractive to the board. I know. I was invisibly serving coffee and Danish as they pored over his CV. . . . Sarah knew Kate's taste – it was essentially the same as her own. Unfortunately it earned Kate an invitation to hit the pavement by three thirty a month ago. So suddenly Sarah had better ditch all she held to be good and true and impress James before she receives an invite to the same street party. Which sounds simple enough. Until you appreciate it's nowhere near as simple as it sounds. . . .
(SAMMY *crosses into the room and sits face to face to* Adam.)
Well, hold on tight. Sarah has to impress James while keeping in mind he's having to second guess the taste of the network script editors – his first point of contact with the powers that be. Men and women whose sole function is to second guess the endlessly mutating tastes of their own heads of department – whose own survival depends on servicing the focus-group predilections of the channel and network Controllers. Near-mythic entities who operate like *Armani* clad black holes, into which all projects are sucked and processed for potential production. These demi-Gods are specialists in one genre, but must now give the thumb up or down across *all*. And so it's not unfair to say that their knowledge of ours is questionable – and conclude that many of them have no greater clue what makes a decent sitcom than – say – (*Picking up a chocolate biscuit*) this. . . . (*Eating the biscuit*) Sarah's locked into a chain of bet-hedging where the only person with a reasonable grasp of what they might actually want is you – and you have no say, and no power whatsoever. You've heard of Catch 22?. . . Double it and you begin to approach where Sarah's standing right now. Approach it, and ask yourself if you want to be a part of it.

An excerpt (abridged) from *A Place at the Table* by Simon Block.
Published by Nick Hern Books, The Glasshouse,
49a Goldhawk Road, London W12 8QP.

RICHARD
mid to late 20s

THE POWER OF THE DOG
Ellen Dryden

First performed at The Orange Tree Theatre, Richmond in 1996.

Vivien Chadwick, Head of the English Department in a failing school run by an incompetent Headmaster, is preparing to take up a new appointment as Head of a school in South London. At the same time she is attempting to move house as well as visit her mother who has suffered a stroke.

In this scene Vivien is in her study talking to Lisa, a problem sixth-former who has turned up late for a tutorial. There is a hammering at the door and RICHARD SHAW storms in. RICHARD is a young teacher who was expecting to take over as Head of English when Vivien left. Always abrasive in manner he is now bitingly angry. Vivien dismisses Lisa. She tells RICHARD she would appreciate it if he refrained from bursting in when she is teaching.

Published by First Writes Publications, London

RICHARD
I want a word with you. Mrs Chadwick. . . .
Oh. I beg your pardon. I was under the impression that School
finished at quarter to four. And your A-level class has shrunk, hasn't
it?. . . Would you mind telling me what the hell you're playing at? I
have just had one of the most humiliating interviews of my life. I was
invited – no summoned – to the Head's office. In writing. For a drink
and a chat after school. I go along expecting to discuss my promo-
tion. Tchah! He really enjoyed himself watching me get the message.
The bit he liked best was telling me this was all done with your
connivance. . . .
I see. You're sorry that he put the boot in before you had the chance.
I'm not one of your half-witted lame ducks. What are you doing
discussing me in this tender fashion behind my back?. . . He's a
contemptible little shit. We all live with that. What I want to know is
why you couldn't tell me to my face – before you went running to
him – that I am totally unfitted to take over from you as Head of the
Department. That you cannot give me any kind of recommendation.
That I am too young. Too *volatile*!!

(*He spits out the word with real venom, but it is obvious that
he is hurt by what he sees as Vivien's betrayal.*)

Oh, it gave him a real thrill sitting there, spreading out his hands and
telling me it was your assessment of me and wouldn't it be better if
I withdrew my application – to avoid embarrassment! For Christ's
sake, Viv, what are you up to? You bloody well appointed me – over
his supine body!. . .

(RICHARD *is stopped in his tracks. He looks at Vivien, conflict-
ing emotions expressing themselves on his face. Finally it is
with an almost comic disgust that he speaks*)

Lying? Oh come on. You must have said something – Even he wouldn't
– Not so blatantly. . . . . . . (*Slowly*) Nevertheless. I can hear you saying
all that about me. . . . You must have said something. What was it? Or
am I not allowed to know?

JIMMIE
American/Los Angeles
late 20s

PULP FICTION
Quentin Tarantino

Pulp Fiction was awarded the Palme d'Or at the Cannes Film Festival in 1994. It was directed by Quentin Tarantino who also plays the part of JIMMIE. It is a trio of stories rotating around the violent misadventures of a collection of outlaws – right out of the pages of pulp fiction.

Jules (black) and Vincent (white) are working for the infamous club owner, Marsellus Wallace. They have a problem. Driving back from a 'job' with Jules' friend Marvin (a young black man) sitting in the back seat, Vincent's '45 goes off accidentally and shoots Marvin in the throat. Before Jules can prevent him, Vincent shoots Marvin again to 'put him out of his misery'. They are left with a headless man and a car that looks like a 'portable slaughterhouse'. They need a 'friendly place' as soon as possible. Jules phones his friend, JIMMIE and asks if they can use his garage for a couple of hours.

In this scene Jules and Vincent are drinking coffee in JIMMIE's kitchen. JIMMIE, a young man in his late twenties is dressed in a bath-robe. He is not at all happy about the situation. His wife will be back in an hour and a half and they've got to be out by then.

Published by Faber & Faber, London

JIMMIE

Knock it off, Julie. . . . I'm not a cob of corn, so you can stop butterin'
me up. I don't need you to tell me how good my coffee is. I'm the
one who buys it, I know how fuckin' good it is. When Bonnie goes
shoppin', she buys shit. I buy the gourmet expensive stuff 'cause
when I drink it, I wanna taste it. But what's on my mind at this
moment isn't the coffee in my kitchen, it's the dead nigger in my
garage. . . . - I'm talkin'. Now let me ask you a question, Jules. When
you drove in here, did you notice a sign out front said, 'Dead Nigger
Storage?'

(Jules starts to 'Jimmie' him -)

. . . answer the question. Did you see a sign out in front of my house
that said, 'Dead Nigger Storage?'. . .You know why you didn't see that
sign?. . . 'Cause storin' dead niggers ain't my fuckin' business!

(Jules starts to 'Jimmie' him.)

. . . I ain't through! Now don't you understand that if Bonnie comes
home and finds a dead body in her house, I'm gonna get divorced.
No marriage counselor, no trial separation - fuckin' divorced. And I
don't wanna get fuckin' divorced. The last time me an' Bonnie talked
about this shit was gonna be the last time me an' Bonnie talked about
this shit. Now I wanna help ya out Julie, I really do. But I ain't gonna
lose my wife doin' it. . . . - don't fuckin' Jimmie me, man, I can't be
Jimmied. There's nothin' you can say that's gonna make me forget I
love my wife. Now she's workin' the graveyard shift at the hospital.
She'll be comin' home in less than an hour and a half. Make your
phone calls, talk to your people, then get the fuck out of my house.
Phone's in my bedroom. . . . *(to himself)* Yeah, yeah, yeah, yeah,
yeah. I'm a real good friend. Good friend, bad husband, soon to be
ex-husband.

THE WOLF
American/Los Angeles

PULP FICTION
Quentin Tarantino

Pulp Fiction was awarded the Palme d'Or at the Cannes Film Festival in 1994. It is a trio of stories rotating around the violent misadventures of a collection of outlaws – right out of the pages of pulp fiction.

Jules and Vincent are two such 'outlaws' working for the infamous club owner, Marsellus Wallace. They have a problem. Driving back from a 'job' with Jules' friend Marvin in the back seat, Vincent's '45 accidentally goes off and shoots Marvin in the throat. Vincent shoots Marvin again to 'put him out of his misery' and they are left with a headless body in a car that looks like 'a portable slaughterhouse'. They drive over to Vincent's friend Jimmie, who most definitely doesn't want to be involved, but allows them to phone Marsellus. Marsellus arranges to send over THE WOLF to solve their problem.

Next morning a silver Porsche draws up outside. Jimmie opens the door. A tuxedo-clad man stands in the doorway, note-book in hand. It is WINSTON WOLF.

Published by Faber & Faber, London

THE WOLF
(*Looks down to his notebook, then up at Jimmie.*)
You're Jimmie, right? This is your house?. . . (*sticks his hand out*) I'm Winston Wolf, I solve problems. . . . May I come in?
(*Jules and Vincent stand up.*)
You must be Jules, which would make you Vincent. Let's get down to brass tacks, gentlemen. If I was informed correctly, the clock is ticking, is that right, Jimmie?. . . Your wife, Bonnie . . . (*refers to his pad*) . . . comes home at 9:30 in the A.M., is that correct?. . . I was led to believe if she comes home and finds us here, she wouldn't appreciate it none too much. . . . That gives us forty minutes to get the fuck outta Dodge, which, if you do what I say when I say it, should be plenty. Now you got a corpse in a car, minus a head, in a garage. Take me to it.
(*Int. Jimmie's Garage – The three men hang back as* THE

WOLF *examines the car in silence.*)
Jimmie?. . . Do me a favor, will ya? Thought I smelled some coffee in there. Would you make me a cup?. . . Lotsa cream, lotsa sugar.
(Jimmie exits. THE WOLF continues his examination.)
. . .About the car, is there anything I need to know? Does it stall, does it make a lot of noise, does it smoke, is there gas in it, anything?. . . Positive? Don't let me out on the road and I find the brake lights don't work. . . . Good enough, let's go back to the kitchen.
(Int. Kitchen – Jimmie hands THE WOLF a cup of coffee.)
Thank you, Jimmie.
(He takes a sip, then nods to Jimmie indicating that the coffee is good. Pacing as he thinks.)
. . . Okay, first thing, you two (*meaning Jules and Vincent*) take the body, stick it in the trunk. Now Jimmie, this looks to be a pretty domesticated house. That would lead me to believe that in the garage or under the sink, you got a bunch of cleaners and cleansers and shit like that, am I correct?. . . Good. What I need you two fellas to do is take those cleaning products and clean the inside of the car. And I'm talkin' fast, fast, fast. You need to go in the back seat, scoop up all those little pieces of brain and skull. Get it out of there. Wipe down the upholstery – now, when it comes to upholstery, it don't need to be spic and span, you don't need to eat off it. Give it a good once over. What you need to take care of are the really messy parts. The pools of blood that have collected, you gotta soak that shit up. But the windows are a different story. Them you really clean. Get the Windex, do a good job. Now Jimmie, we need to raid your linen closet. I need blankets, I need comforters, I need quilts, I need bedspreads. The thicker the better, the darker the better. No whites, can't use 'em. We need to camouflage the interior of the car. We're gonna line the front seat and the back seat and the floorboards with quilts and blankets. If a cop stops us and starts stickin' his big snout in the car, the subterfuge won't last. But at a glance, the car will appear to be normal. Jimmie – lead the way, boys – get to work.
(THE WOLF and Jimmie turn, heading for the bedroom, leaving Vincent and Jules standing in the kitchen. . . . THE WOLF stops and turns around.)
Get it straight, Buster. I'm not here to say 'please'. I'm here to tell you what to do. And if self-preservation is an instinct you possess, you better fuckin' do it and do it quick. I'm here to help. If my help's not appreciated, lotsa luck gentlemen. . . . If I'm curt with you, it's because time is a factor. I think fast, I talk fast and I need you guys to act fast if you want to get out of this. So pretty please, with sugar on top, clean the fuckin' car.

STARBUCK
Western USA
30

THE RAINMAKER
N. Richard Nash

Produced at the St Martin's Theatre, London in 1956 and revived in the States in the 1990s, it is set on a ranch in a Western state of the U.S.A. on a summer's day.

A terrible drought is killing the Curry family's livestock and then BILL STARBUCK appears, as if from nowhere, announcing that he can bring them rain. H. C. Curry, head of the family, is prepared to try anything and so is his younger son, Jim, but his older son, Noah, and daughter, Lizzie, distrust this stranger.

In this scene H. C. asks STARBUCK to explain how he intends to make this rain.

Published by Samuel French, London

STARBUCK

One hundred dollars in advance – and inside of twenty-four hours you'll have rain. . . . Rain is rain, brother. It comes from the sky. It's a wetness known as water. *Aqua pura*. Mammals drink it, fish swim in it, little boys wade in it, and birds flap their wings and sing like sunrise. Water! (*He picks up the pitcher from the table and pours some water over his head*) I recommend it. . . . What do you care how I do it, sister, as long as it's done? But I'll tell you how I'll do it. I'll lift this stick and take a long swipe at the sky and let down a shower of hailstones as big as canteloupes. I'll shout out some good old Nebraska cusswords and there's a lake where your corral used to be. Or I'll just sing a little tune, maybe, and it'll sound so pretty and sound so sad you'll weep and your old man will weep and the sky will get all misty-like and shed the prettiest tears you ever did see. How'll I do it? Girl, I'll just do it. . . . Sister, the last place I brought rain is now called Starbuck – they named it after me. Dry? I tell you, those people didn't have enough damp to blink their eyes. So I get out my big wheel and my rolling drum and my yella hat with the three little feathers in it. I look up at the sky and I say: 'Cumulus,' I say: 'Cumulo-nimbus. Nimbulo-cumulus.' And pretty soon – way up there – there's a teeny little cloud the size of a mare's tail – and then over there – there's another cloud lookin' like a white-washed chicken coop. And then I look up and all of a sudden there's a herd of white buffalo stampedin' across the sky. And then, sister-of-all-good-people, down comes the rain. (*He crosses to the door* R) Rain in buckets, rain in barrels, fillin' the low-lands, floodin' the gullies. And the land is as green as the valley of Adam. And when I rode out of there I looked behind me and I see the prettiest colours in the sky – green, blue, purple, gold – colours to make you cry. And me? I'm ridin' right through that rainbow. Well, how about it? Is it a deal? (*He crosses to* C. *Getting down to work*) Now – what kind of rain would you like?

JOHN DOE
New York

SEVEN
Andrew Kevin Walker

Seven was released in 1995 and picked up an award for Best Film.

A serial killer, JOHN DOE, is at large. He has a taste for literary allusion, and his victims are butchered in grotesque accordance with the dictates of the Seven Deadly Sins. The cops investigating the case, Somerset, on the verge of retirement, and Mills, a youngster, are at a loss, until the killer walks straight into their hands, giving the film its final horrible twist.

JOHN DOE is now in custody. Five of the deadly sins have been 'atoned' for and there are two more bodies yet to be found. DOE's lawyer says his client will take Detectives Somerset and Mills to see the bodies, but emphasises it must be these two officers only and no one else. If this offer is not accepted he will plead insanity, and owing to the extreme nature of the crimes will most certainly get off. On the other hand, if these conditions are accepted he will sign a full confession and plead guilty.

In this scene in Somerset's car, Somerset is at the wheel, with Mills in the passenger seat, looking back at JOHN DOE through the protective wire in the back seat. Mills remarks that there is nothing unusual about these murders. 'In two months, no one's going to even remember this happened'. DOE looks down for a moment, then looks up, almost shyly, as he begins to speak.

Published by Faber & Faber, London

JOHN DOE
You can't see the whole . . . the whole complete act yet. Not yet. But, when this is done, it's going to be . . . so . . . so . . . . . . It's going to be flawless. People will barely comprehend, but they won't be able to deny it. . . .
   (*Doe looks down, licking his lips. He clenches his hands into fists, digging his fingertips into his sweaty palms.*)

I can't wait for you to see. I can't wait . . . (*pause, looks to Mills*) It's really going to be something. . . . Oh, don't worry . . . . . . you won't miss a thing. . . . It's more comfortable for you . . . to label me insane. . . . It's something I wouldn't expect you to accept . . . but, I didn't choose this. I was chosen. . . . (*long pause*) I . . . I doubt I enjoyed it any more than . . . Detective Mills would enjoy some time alone with me in a room without windows. (*looks to Mills*) Isn't that true? How happy would it make you to hurt me, with impunity. . . . You would-n't because you know there are consequences. It's in those eyes of yours, though . . . nothing wrong with a man taking pleasure in his work. (*pause, shakes his head*) I won't deny my own personal desire to turn each sin against the sinner. I only took their sins to logical conclusions. . . . Look at the people I killed. An obese man, a disgust-ing man who could barely stand up . . . who if you saw him on the street, you'd point so your friends could mock him along with you. Who if you saw him while you were eating, you wouldn't be able to finish your meal. After him I picked the lawyer. And, you both must have been secretly thanking me for that one. This was a man who dedicated his life to making money by lying with every breath he could muster . . . to keeping rapists and murderers on the streets. . . . A woman . . . . . . (*louder*) A woman . . . so ugly on the inside that she couldn't bear to go on living if she couldn't be beauti-ful on the outside. A drug dealer . . . a drug-dealing pederast, actually. (*laughs at that one*) And, don't forget the disease-spreading whore. Only in a world this shitty could you even try to say these were innocent people and keep a straight face. (*getting worked up*) That's the point. You see a deadly sin on almost every street corner, and in every home, literally. And we tolerate it. Because it's common, it seems trivial, and we tolerate, all day long, morning, noon and night. Not anymore. I'm setting the example, and it's going to be puzzled over and studied and followed, from now on. . . . You should be thanking me. . . . You're going to be remembered, and it's all because of me. And, the only reason I'm here right now is because I wanted to be. . . . Don't ask me to pity the people I killed. I don't mourn them any more than I mourn the thousands who died in Sodom and Gomorrah. . . . The Lord works in mysterious ways.

MELCHIOR
late teens

SPRING AWAKENING
Frank Wedekind
A new version by Ted Hughes

First produced in Germany in 1891 and in London at the Royal Court Theatre in 1965. This new version was presented by the Royal Shakespeare Company in The Pit in 1995.

The play deals with the problems of young love and adults' inability to talk about these problems openly with their children. The story revolves around Wendla and Moritz, who pay with their lives for the moral dishonesty of their parents. MELCHIOR is the brightest student in his class. He is Moritz's friend and Wendla's lover. When Moritz commits suicide, a document on sexual reproduction, written in MELCHIOR's handwriting, is found amongst his belongings. Shocked by its contents and looking for an excuse for the suicide, the school authorities blame MELCHIOR and he is expelled. At the same time Wendla's mother finds a letter written by MELCHIOR to her daughter begging her forgiveness for the 'sin' he has committed. MELCHIOR is sent to the Reformatory.

In this scene, MELCHIOR has escaped from the Reformatory and has climbed over the wall into the cemetery. It is a windy, moonlit night.

Published by Faber & Faber, London

MELCHIOR
The pack will never find me here. While they're searching the brothels, I'll get my breath back and take stock. Think what next. Coat ripped to shreds, pockets empty, every living soul ready to point me out and turn me in. When there's light enough, I'll have to find a way through the woods.
That was a cross I knocked over. A night like this, any flowers will be frozen stiff. Bare earth everywhere. The land of the dead.

Climbing through that skylight was nothing to this. I'm not sure I was quite ready for this.

Like the roof of the abyss. Holes in the earth. Everything sinking away in front of me – Why didn't I stay where I was?

Why should she bear the punishment for what was my crime? Why don't I bear it? That's why they call providence inscrutable. I would have broken stones, starved myself –

What keeps me going? Something. One crime drops you through to the next. I'm condemned to the lowest sludge. Too weak even to put an end to it.

But I wasn't evil. I was not evil. I was not evil.

No living person wandering among graves ever felt such envy – to be down among them. Ah, but I haven't the guts. If only I could be insane enough. If only I could go just briefly mad – tonight. The new graves are over there. I should take a look. The wind plays in a different key on each headstone. Dismal symphony! The wreaths disintegrate and bits hang dangling on strings over the faces of stones. Like a forest of scarecrows. On every grave a scarecrow, each one more horrible than the last – faces looming like housefronts, frightening off the devils. That gleaming gold lettering looks very bleak. And that's the weeping willow groaning. Leafy fingers stroking the epitaphs.

And now a praying cherub. And an engraved slab.

The shadow of a cloud. It pours across the heavens. It seems to howl silently. It boils and piles up out of the east, like a vast military campaign. Not a star to be seen.

Evergreen around this one. Evergreen – a girl.

> Here rests in God
> Wendla Bergman
> Born 5 May 1878
> died of anaemia
> 27 October 1892
> Blessed are the pure in heart

I killed her. Her murderer – me! No point in crying here. I must get out. I must get away from this place. Get away –

SUSLOV
42

SUMMERFOLK
Maxim Gorky
A new version by Nick Dear

This version was first performed in the Olivier auditorium of the Royal National Theatre in 1999.

In the early years of the twentieth century, Russians of every social class were beginning to sense the onset of a great upheaval. A diverse group of Russians meet, as they do every year, at their Summer holiday retreat. Some are frightened at the prospect of change, some are angry and some yearn for a new life. As they question the value of their work, their art and their leisure, relationships break under the strain and scandals of business and infidelity are laid bare.

SUSLOV describes himself as a 'provincial Russian philistine'. He enjoys a drink with his friend, Bassov, and a game of chess at the club. In this scene, set in a clearing in front of the Bassov's dacha, Bassov's sister-in-law, Kaleria, is reading one of her poems. Her brother, Vlass, a young man who feels obliged to turn everything into a joke, insists on reciting a poem he has just made up to the assembled company. In it he refers to them all as 'worthless people' dithering like 'headless chickens'. SUSLOV is furious. Everyone knows that Vlass is influenced by his infatuation for Maria Lvovna and her socialist ideals, and SUSLOV addresses his reply to her.

(A 'dacha' is a Russian country cottage used especially in summer.)

Published by Faber & Faber, London

SUSLOV

Will you allow me, as a representative of the headless chickens' faction, to reply to that . . . that hellish . . . it doesn't even have a literary genre! But I shan't address my critique to you, Vlass. Oho no. I shall address the source and fount of your inspiration: Maria Lvovna. . . . Everyone knows you're the muse of this poet, that your hand holds his – pen – as he writes. . . . don't interrupt, you! – Maria Lvovna, you are, I gather, an idealist. You'd have us believe you're involved in secret plots and programmes, lots of cloak-and-dagger stuff, turning the tide of history et cetera. Well, perhaps you are. Doesn't concern me. But you evidently think that this subversive activity gives you an automatic right to sneer at people. . . . You preach at us incessantly. You've taken this tuneless youth and orchestrated him to a pitch of denunciation. . . . If we don't live our lives in quite the way you would wish, perhaps we have our reasons. Every single one of us here knew poverty in our youth. We all remember what it's like to be hungry. Is it not natural that, in our maturity, we like a good meal and a drink? The chance to take it easy? Aren't we entitled to some recompense, for all the hardship we grew up with?. . . We are the children of workers and tradesmen. We went bloody hungry! Did we not? Who will contradict me? It may not be quite to your socialist taste, Maria Lvovna, but we *deserve* our little luxuries, it's natural, it's human nature! Hell's bells, human nature is paramount, and then comes all the other shit! So why don't you leave us in peace? You can criticise us, you can bait others to criticise us, you can call us cowards, hypocrites, but none of us is going to suddenly start doing social work! Not one! Not one of us!. . . No, to hell with it, I won't stop! And as for me, yes, as for me, let's consider me for a change – I'm no infant. I've grown up. I don't need teachers any longer, thank you, Maria Lvovna. I'm a grown-up Russian man, a common-or-garden Russian man, a philistine if you like. Yes, a provincial Russian philistine, no more nor less! And here is my programme: I shall carry on being a philistine, and I shall do whatever the bloody hell I want! To sum up: I shit on your slogans. And your revolution.

VLASS
25

SUMMERFOLK
Maxim Gorky
A new version by Nick Dear

This version was first performed in the Olivier auditorium of the Royal National Theatre in 1999.

In the early years of the twentieth century, Russians of every social class were beginning to sense the onset of a great upheaval. A diverse group of Russians meet, as they do every year, at their Summer holiday retreat. Some are frightened at the prospect of change, some are angry and some yearn for a new life. As they question the value of their work, their art and their leisure, relationships break under the strain and scandals of business and infidelity are laid bare.

VLASS works as a lawyer's clerk. Dissatisfied with his life, he feels obliged to turn everything into a joke, much to everyone's annoyance. In this scene it is early evening and VLASS comes along the path from the woods accompanied by Maria Lvovna and Kiril Dudakov. He is describing his early life, making light of a wretched childhood when he was beaten by a drunken father.

Published by Faber & Faber, London

VLASS
My father was a cook. Potentially a very creative man. But he drank too hard. His love for me was somewhat severe. So severe, I was dragged everywhere he went. He had to travel to find work. Which meant his marriage to my mother was . . . problematic. Once in a while I'd run home to her, but he'd come steaming round to the laundry, batter his way in, crack a few heads, and put me back to work in the kitchens. Meanwhile he developed the lethal notion that I should be educated. This happened whilst he was working for a bishop, so in short order I was installed in theological school. A few months later, fired again, he went to work for the railroad, so I found myself in technical college. Then it was agriculture. Then art school, followed by business administration, at which I proved less than a runaway success, and was consequently thrashed. And put back to work in the kitchens. To sum up: by the time I was seventeen, I had such a deeply ingrained aversion to learning anything at all, that even the rudiments of smoking were beyond me. Why do you look at me like that, Maria Lvovna?. . . Sad? Well, thankfully, it's ended.

ODYSSEUS

TANTALUS
John Barton

First performed at the Denver Center for the Performing Arts, Denver, Colorado in October 2000 and transferred to the Barbican Theatre, London in May 2001 after a short tour.

Tantalus is an epic tale of the Trojan War, described as 'a crusade which becomes a catastrophe.' It is divided into three parts, *The Outbreak of War*, *The War*, and *The Homecoming*, and is made up of ten plays, one of which is *Odysseus*.

In this play Troy has been overthrown, King Priam slain and Queen Hecuba and the Trojan women taken captive. ODYSSEUS has treated the women kindly and with respect but is unable to prevent the sacrifice of Hecuba's daughter, Polyxena, who has been chosen by Neoptomelus, brutal killer of Priam, as the 'war prize' for his dead father, Achilles.

In this scene, Polyxena is being prepared for sacrifice, as Neoptolemus enters. He accuses her of betraying Achilles to his death and demands that she take off her dress and wears the yellow dress his sister, Hesione wore when he killed her. When she refuses he threatens to tear it off her. ODYSSEUS intervenes, reprimanding Neoptolemus, for trying to humiliate Polyxena.

Published by Oberon Books, London

ODYSSEUS
That would be unworthy
Of you and of your father:
Don't do it, Neoptolemus.
Is this the way to treat
Your own father's wife?
I cannot prevent you
From shedding this girl's blood
Since Achilles' ghost commands it,
But if you also try
To humiliate Polyxena
It is you who will be humiliated
And held in contempt
For the rest of your mortal life.
Already in the army
Some speak of you with horror.
When you first came to Troy
You were clean and pure and noble;
Now you are soiled and polluted.
You must listen once again
To the spirit of truth inside you
Or the rest of your life be wretched.
Are you not ashamed
Somewhere inside you?. . .
Let me speak to you for a moment
As I once spoke to your father.
Let me remind you
How it was with the old heroes
When passion overtook them:
At times they also turned
Into monsters as you have,
But they overcame their wrath
As your father did and you must
If you wish to be thought a hero.
Men like their heroes to be noble,
Or at least to act nobly.

ERNEST JOBELIN
young

THE THREESOME
Eugene Labiche
Translated by Neil Bartlett

Originally presented in Paris as *Les Plus Heureux des Trois* in 1870, this translation by Neil Bartlett was performed under the title of *The Threesome* at the Lyric Theatre, Hammersmith in March 2000.

The action takes place in Paris in 1870 and tells the story of the adulterous adventures of a suburban couple, Alphonse Marjavel and his wife Hermance. ERNEST JOBELIN is Alphonse's best friend and Hermance's lover. Misreading a secret signal from Hermance he has climbed up the balcony to her window, only to find that Alphonse has retired to bed early with stomach cramp and is calling for him. ERNEST is obliged to spend the night in the living room in case his 'best friend' should need him.

In this scene ERNEST has been woken up by Hermance to tell him that her husband is much better. He is still clutching a piece of broken drainpipe that came off in his hand as he climbed up to her window. He complains bitterly about husbands.

Published by Oberon Books, London

ERNEST
Husbands! Life of bloody Riley!!. . . Oh, I know there is the one slight
drawback . . . but it seems to be one they're perfectly happy to
overlook. Apart from that, what's their problem? We cosset them, we
coddle them, we bend over backwards to keep them comfy – plump,
rosy-cheeked, cheerful souls, full of the joys of spring, not to mention
of themselves – and meanwhile we, we mere adulterers, we're skin
and bone – jealous – jumpy – guilty . . . obliged to behave like . . .
like we were doing something wrong. . . . For them, dinner's always
ready, the table's always laid, service comes with a smile; while we,
we have to hide in sofas and mount drainpipes just to scavenge the
leftovers – when they feel like leaving us any! . . . Ah! I don't see why
they have to make our lives so difficult. (*He sits down on the little
chair stage left.*) And, to add insult to injury, your husband thinks I'm
stupid! Stupid . . . but loyal . . . . . . I beg your pardon Madame but he
did say that at twenty-seven minutes past three – my watch keeps
excellent time. (*He looks for his watch but it is missing.*) Oh – I
must have left it by the bed . . . 'Stupid, but loyal' . . . and you said
nothing to the contrary . . . on the contrary – . . . (Hermance *comes
to sit near him. Having let slip a small sigh, he turns gently and
gets on his knees in front of her.*) . . . Do you know this is the first
time I've had you all to myself in two months?. . . (*He takes her by
the waist.*) So . . . . . . So this seems the perfect opportunity for a
quick chat. A quick . . . intimate conversation. A quick –
  (*The sound of* Jobelin *sneezing in the room next door.*)
. . . Jesus Christ! . . .
  (Hermance *exits midstage right.*)
ERNEST (*Alone, buttoning up his jacket.*) Right . . . time to face the
music . . . it'll be a relief, frankly; I've had enough of all these gymnas-
tics, not to mention the hysterics. (*Imitating Hermance's voice.*)
'We're lost!' – 'We're saved!' – 'We're lost!' – . . . (*Opening the midstage
right door.*) Sir, I am at your disposal.

'OLD' JOBELIN
middle-aged

THE THREESOME
Eugene Labiche
Translated by Neil Bartlett

Originally presented in Paris as *Les Plus Heureux des Trois* in 1870, this translation by Neil Bartlett was performed under the title of *The Threesome* at the Lyric Theatre, Hammersmith in March 2000.

The action takes place in Paris in 1870 and tells the story of the adulterous adventures of a suburban couple, Alphonse Marjaval and his wife Hermance. It is Alphonse's birthday and 'OLD' JOBELIN enters carrying a bottle and a bouquet of roses. JOBELIN is the uncle of Alphonse's best friend, Ernest and is described as an ex-adulterer, having been the lover of Alphonse's first wife, Melanie. He is met by the maid, Petunia. As she goes off to announce his arrival, he puts the bottle and the bouquet on the sofa and crosses over to the portrait of Hermance hanging on the wall by the door. He starts to talk to it and then turns it over to reveal the face of Melanie.

Published by Oberon Books, London

JOBELIN

(*Entering upstage with a bottle and a bouquet of roses.*)
Is M. Marjavel in?. . .

(*The maid goes out*)

(*He puts the bottle and bouquet down on the sofa.*) I've come to
wish Marjavel many happy; a habit I got into in the days of his dear
departed first wife. . . . Oh dear I still can't come in here without
feeling moved . . . Just one swift melancholy shufty at poor Melanie
(*He talks to the portrait of Hermance.*) You've been replaced,
I'm afraid, old girl!. . . forgotten, and so quickly – barely a year and
three days. . . . 'The funeral baked meats, scarce cold upon the table,
etc. . . .'. . . (*Going up to the portrait and looking at it.*) But I'm
still here, and I . . . (*Stopping.*) Oh, no, that's the second one. . . . (*He
turns the portrait round to Melanie's side.*) But I'm still here, observ-
ing my melancholy pilgrimage. . . . Melanie, darling . . . we were so
very naughty . . . (*Talking to the matching portrait of Marjavel.*) We
deceived you, Marjavel . . . you good man!. . . You good, good man
. . . you bloody perfect man you. . . . Still, no regrets; sorry, and all
that . . . (*He comes back centre stage.*) And actually I'm only sorry
she's not around any more . . . 'cause now she's not . . . poor old
thing . . .!; it was my idea, Marjavel sticking her on the back of the
new one. . . . The last time we saw each other, it was in a cab . . . she
was so worried about being spotted – touching, really – used to hide
behind this fan . . . Poor old thing . . . memories everywhere . . . (*He
sighs as he looks at the sofa, then goes to the mantelpiece.*) It was
my idea to give Marjavel the stag's head, for his birthday. Rather a
Machiavellian touch, I thought – we used to use it as our postbox.
(*He opens it.*) Grief! a letter!. . . must be an old one that's got stuck
in there somehow. (*He opens the letter, and comes centre stage.*)
How very careless!. . . very shaky handwriting – she always was a bit
of a trembler. (*Reading.*) 'We are in great danger . . . the cab-driver
recognised us, he's spying on us; license number 2114. Do try and
have a word with him . . . you know carrying on in cabs always gives
me presentiments'. She always used to get a bit girly when she felt
one of her presentiments coming on . . . dreamt about a black cat
once and quite convinced herself it was a Chief Superintendent.

(*The maid enters to fetch him.*)

(*Picking up his bottle and bouquet.*) Ah, splendid – I've got him a
bunch of roses and a bottle of Lafitte 1789 – only one of its kind,
apparently – (*He exits.*)

LANCE
mid 30s

TOAST
Richard Bean

First performed at the Royal Court Theatre Upstairs in 1999 and set in 1975 in a Yorkshire bread plant.

It is the Sunday shift. Seven men come together to bake enough bread to feed the population of Hull. The ovens are cranked up and running, but there's a spanner in the works which threatens bread production in Hull, and life as they know it for the men on the shift. One of the team is on holiday and LANCE BISHOP, who announces that he is a mature student studying sociology and history, has been sent to replace him. LANCE's wrists are badly scarred and the men soon come to the conclusion that he is from 'a medical institution of some sort'.

In this scene Walter Nelson, the mixer – know as 'Nellie' – is taking a break. LANCE comes into the canteen carrying Nellie's vest which he's rescued from the mix. He sits down opposite Nellie and asks him for a cigarette.

Published by Oberon Books, London

LANCE
Would it be possible to touch you for a cigarette?. . . I normally eschew the weed, on health grounds naturally, but in situations like this the pressure of social conformity is greater than my will to live.
  (Nellie, *with great difficulty, releases a cigarette, and lights it for him.*)
. . . I'm not a student Walter. I'm not at school. I'm here to see you. I can't tell you Walter, being dead has made a significant difference to my life. I have no concerns about my health, and I groom less. (*Beat.*) It is very opportune for me – being 'on a smoke' whilst you are taking your half hour. Alone in the canteen. It is quite perfect. One might even say designed. I feared that I would have to corner you in the lavatory or steal thirty seconds in the mixing room, just to be with you.

(Pause.)

Are you prepared Walter?. . .That is exactly what I said! How can one prepare? Death is the only real adventure. Planning, preparation, making ready – all tosh! A willing acquiescence with fate is all that one can reasonably contribute. *(Beat.)* I have told them but they take very little notice of me. I said take him, snatch him away, suddenly. Why go to the expense of sending a messenger? Do you realise, Walter, to send me here has required eight signatures on two separate requisitions. One for the exceptional expenditure incurred, and one for a four-day visa. . . . I'm from the other side. From across the metaphorical water. . . . The land of living souls and rotting bodies. The next world. . . . Ah! It is true that I am chosen for this role because I am, so I understand, perceived to be mildly eccentric, but that is functional. The living dismiss me as a madman, leaving only my clients to take me seriously. And you, Walter, are a client. . . . I'm a messenger. Your time is up, Walter. They've made a decision at last. An all-night meeting. A compromise solution was suggested which, though not ideal, did not damage the long-term objectives of either party. There's a place for you now. Provision has been made. Your er . . . loyalty to this company, and all-round contribution to society, albeit in the narrow area of bread mass production, served you well. The committee actually calculated how many loaves you've mixed in the forty-five years you've worked here. Two hundred and twenty million. That's an awful lot of toast Walter!. . .Trust me, it's not as terrible as it sounds. I know where you're going. It's not perfect, but it could be worse. Let's just say, there are more ovens here – comprenez?. . .You are going to die Walter. Tonight. It'll be quick, and, thankfully, there'll be hardly any mess.

(LANCE *stands, collects his things together and exits.*)

BUKS
South African
aged 76

VALLEY SONG
Athol Fugard

First performed at the Royal Court Theatre Downstairs in January 1996. This play is about the fears, hopes and dreams of the people in a new South Africa, and is set in a small village in the Sneuberg Mountains.

Abraam Jonkers, known as BUKS, ex-corporal in the famous Coloured regiment, the Cape Corps, worries about the Whiteman buying the old Landman house and taking over the piece of land – his 'akkers'. His granddaughter, Veronica, dreams of eventually leaving the village and going to Johannesburg to study singing. BUKS looks after his granddaughter on his own, her mother having run away when she was nearly the same age as Veronica is now.

In this scene he is alone talking to his dead wife, Betty.

Note: the roles of the Author (aged early sixties) and BUKS are played by the same actor.

Published by Faber & Faber, London

BUKS

So, Betty . . . what do you think? (*A pause* . . . *he remembers.*) 'Speak, woman, I can see there are thoughts in your head!' (*Shakes his head.*) Ja, if only it was still like that and we could sit down at the kitchen table tonight and talk about things the way we used to. More and more I feel so useless . . . so by myself . . .! There's nobody I want to talk to anymore – only Veronica, and I can't put my worries on those young shoulders, specially when she is one of them. Am I saying the right things to her, Betty? Doing the right things?

You can see for yourself she is happy. She is singing more than ever – even making her own songs now. And obedient. She listens to me. When I tell her to do something she does it. But I can also see she is starting to get restless. She's nearly as old now as Caroline was when she ran away. And she looks so much like her, Betty, it really does frighten me. Just yesterday she was standing in the street laughing and teasing a young man, her hands on her hips just the way her mother used to do it. I thought I was seeing a ghost. Because it was Caroline standing there! So waar! I nearly called her name. Sometimes it happens in the house as well, when she's sweeping, or doing the washing . . . I see Caroline! But then she starts singing and I remember . . . No! It's Veronica. It's my grandchild.

And now there is also this Whiteman looking at the house and the land. He is going to buy, Betty, I know it. And then what do I do? I know what you want to say . . . Have faith in the Lord, Abraam Jonkers . . . and I do . . . it's just that He's asking for a lot of it these days.

DIGGIE WHEELER
Rural Warwickshire
approx 60s

A WARWICKSHIRE TESTIMONY
April De Angelis

First performed by the Royal Shakespeare Company at The Other Place, Stratford-Upon-Avon in 1999.

The action takes place in a small Warwickshire village and is written around the 'testimonies' of members of local communities who were invited to contribute memories and impressions of past and present experiences. We see the past with the 'big house', the servant class and the close-knit family ties of a bygone generation, and the present with its eye to big business, where nothing stays the same for long and the 'quaintness' of the cottages is all that remains of the old village life.

DIGGIE WHEELER's character weaves its way throughout the play. As a child he sustained brain damage from a blow from a falling tree, which his mother says left him with the gift of second sight. When war broke out and other young men were called up, he was sent to work in an abattoir. In this scene he is wandering alone in the woods talking to himself, and 'sees' the murder of a young girl.

Published by Faber & Faber, London

DIGGIE

I sleep in this wood sometimes. I sleep where I can. I like the smell of the earth. I clear weeds away sometimes but nobody can see. They come back quick enough, but I like the work. In the other place I didn't like it. The bodies came too fast. Swinging towards you another and another. Stab, slit. Stab, slit. Then another. Swinging away, swing towards you. Your feet in the blood. The stink. Pigs screaming, machines shrilling. In twenty seconds they've bled to death. You know what's coming towards you; a death and another and another and your heart shuts off. That's your bit of peace. It's peaceful here. Except when he comes. I don't like to see him. I don't like to see him with the girl. He has her by the arm and he pulls her. She is talking to him all the while but he's not listening. She's a pretty girl. I found an orchid here that's very rare. You don't see them much. Like a single white flame balancing on its stalk. Things have gone. Things you saw every day. Flowers. Primroses. They used to be every-where. Birds have gone too. It's quieter in the woods. Maybe they all flew away one winter and decided not to come back. I might have done that if I was a bird. She's saying to him to let her go. But he's not. She's white. Her face is white and her hair is stuck to it dark like weeds. He has her by the arm and he's not letting go. He has a coat on like a soldier's so it's harder to make him out, but her white face sticks out. There she is. There's the orchid. She's still there.

(He gets down to look.)

I could watch her all day. White lady we used to call her. Nobody comes here. Nobody should hurt you. Army green. I can see him now. She fights him but he has a knife. Please stop. Please. Then it gets dark. All the while the white lady glows in the dark like a flame. By her it's peaceful.

FINBAR
Irish
late 40s

THE WEIR
Conor McPherson

First performed at The Royal Court Theatre Upstairs in 1997 and then at the Duke of York's Theatre, London in 1998.

The action takes place in present time in a bar in a rural part of Ireland - Northwest Leitrim or Sligo. Barman, Brendon, and locals, FINBAR, Jack and Jim, are swapping ghost stories to impress Valerie, a young woman from Dublin newly moved into the area. FINBAR has a wedding to cater for the next day and in this speech is talking about the bride, Nuala, who used to work for him as a chambermaid.

Published by Nick Hern Books, London

FINBAR

Ah, no, no, no. I'm just watching the time. We've a wedding tomorrow.
. . . No there's certain things I do myself on a big day. One of the first
things I ever learned in the business. The importance of good stock. .
. . For the soup. For the gravy, for the sauces, ah, you use it all over the
place. And it's just a little thing I do. A little ritual. In the morning, I help
do the stock. What do we have from yesterday and so on. A little mad
thing I do, but there you are. . . . Ah, it's a little thing I do. Little super-
stition. These'll tell you. I'm famous for it. . . . Do you know Nuala
Donnelly? 'Nu' they call her. She used to work for me in the Arms.
Declan Donnelly's girl. Gas young one. . . . You used to be pals with
Declan, Jim. . . . She's a gas young one, the daughter. 'Nu' they call her.
'Call me Nu,' she says, the first day she was working for me. Not afraid
to speak up for herself or anything. Used to tell us who was having
affairs and all this. She was a chambermaid, you see. She knew the
couples who were being all illicit because she'd go in to do the room
in the morning and the bed would be already made. The woman in the
affair would have done it out of guilt, you see. Cover it all up, for
herself as much as for anyone else. She's a mad young one. . . .
She's a gabber and a talker. . . . She is getting married to some fella
from out the country. He must be in his forties. Shame, a young one
getting hitched to an auld fell like that. He must have plenty of money.
(To Valerie, *indicating* Jack.) Be like getting married to that. He's a
nice stash hidden away in that little garage. I'll tell you. Hoping to
trap some little thing with it. Isn't that right, Jack?. . . But you want
to be careful of the old lads living on their own. They've a big pot
of stew constantly on the heat, and they just keep throwing a few
bits of scraps in it every couple of days. And they'd survive on that,
don't you Jack? That'd do you?. . . Aw. Dreadful fellas. And then they
manage to get a girl and the dust'd be like that on everything. And
your man'd be after living in two rooms all his life, and the poor
young one would have to get in and clean it all out. Thirty years of
old newspapers and cheap thrillers, all lying there in a damp since
their mammies died and that was the last bit of cleaning went on in
the place. That right Jack?. . . Oh, they'd be desperate men. Changing
the sheets in the bed every Christmas. And there'd be soot all over
everything, and bits of rasher, and egg and pudding on the floor. . . .
(*winks at* Valerie). Sure I'm only telling like it is, ha?

An excerpt (abridged) from *The Weir* by Conor McPherson.
Published by Nick Hern Books, The Glasshouse,
49a Goldhawk Road, London W12 8QP.

USEFUL ADDRESSES

The Academy Drama School,
189 Whitechapel Road,
London, E1 1DN
Tel: 020 7377 8735

The Actors'Theatre School,
32 Exeter Road,
London, NW2 4SB
Tel: 020 8450 0371

Penny Dyer,
Dialect Coach
Tel: 020 8543 2946

Barry Grantham
806 Howard House
Dolphin Square
London SW1V 3PQ
Tel: 020 7798 8246

The Guildhall School of Music and Drama,
Barbican,
London, EC2Y 8DT
Tel: 020 7628 2571

London Academy of Music and Dramatic Art (LAMDA)
Tower House,
226 Cromwell Road,
London, SW5 0SR
Tel: 020 7373 9883

Offstage Theatre and Film Bookshop,
37 Chalk Farm Road,
London, NW1 8AJ
Tel: 020 7485 4996

Royal Academy of Dramatic Art,
62/64 Gower Street,
London, WC1E 6ED
Tel: 020 7636 7076

Spotlight, (*Casting Directory* and *Contacts*)
7 Leicester Place,
London, WC2H 7BP
Tel: 020 7437 7631

COPYRIGHT HOLDERS